EMILY GWATHMEY AND ELLEN STERN

Sister Sets

Sisters Whose Togetherness Sets Them Apart

WILLIAM MORROW AND COMPANY, INC. NEW YORK

Library of Congress Cataloging-in-Publication Data

Gwathmey, Emily Margolin.
    Sister sets: sisters whose togetherness sets them apart / Emily Gwathmey and Ellen Stern.—1st ed.
        p.   cm.
    Includes index
    ISBN 0-688-15331-3 (alk. paper)
    1. Sisters. 2. Sisters—Family relationships. I. Stern, Ellen Stock.
II. Title.
BF723.S43G93   1997
306.875′4—dc21

Printed in the United States of America

First Edition

1 2 3 4 5 6 7 8 9 10

BOOK DESIGN BY LEAH S. CARLSON

This book is dedicated

to our own dear sisters, here and there

CONTENTS

SISTER DEAREST

Top: *Barbara, Emily, Laura, and Janet Margolin*
Above: *Ellen and Bonnie Stock*
Opposite: *Three little sailor girls of yesteryear*

We are both sisters, and we are both blessed.

I, Emily, am the second-born of a set of twins (in China, I'd be considered the first), and we—it's always been we—are the oldest of four girls. Barbara and I (the twins), Janet (was she in the middle of four, or was I?), and little Laura, the last, grew up in a ten-room apartment in Manhattan overlooking the Central Park reservoir with art and nature in full surround.

I, Ellen, am the older one. Carol (whom I promptly nicknamed Bonnie in honor of my best friend at nursery school, and who has never forgiven me) and I grew up in New Haven, in a ten-room shingled Victorian house with lawns, porches, big trees, a grapevine, and a memorable hammock for reading and swinging.

As sisters in a set, we were fascinated by the emotional complexity of our sisterness—and everybody else's. Sisterhood is a love-hate roundelay, with iridescent levels of attachment. Laced with love, fraught with ambiguity, tainted by envy, the relationship is elastic and enduring. Because we view the same events at the same time from different perspectives, we are able to help one another remember, interpret, invent and even reinvent family history.

Our lives teemed with sister teams. I, Emily, was

intrigued by the Elliott twins at school; they were identical, and we were not. I, Ellen, kept a keen eye on the Osterweis twins across the street; the only way to tell them apart was that one dressed in pink and the other in blue. When Bonnie and I were asked if *we* were twins (which happened often, although we were three and a half years apart), we were thrilled.

The stories we read were resplendent with sisters—"Snow White and Rose Red," "The Twelve Dancing Princesses," Alice escaping from her older sister down the rabbit hole to Wonderland, and Anne Frank, who was unable to escape from her older sister—or, tragically, anyone else. But of them all, the most significant for me, Emily, were the four March girls in *Little Women*, the three Fossil sisters in Noel Streatfeild's shoe series, the look-alike *Flicka, Ricka, and Dicka* from Sweden, and Charlotte and Emily (!) in Rumer Godden's *The Doll's House*.

Cinderella and her wicked stepsisters sparked the musical, *Drudgella*, that I, Ellen, wrote one Connecticut summer. All the parts—the grimy heroine, the treacherous Myrna and Melva, the cruel stepmother, the fairy godmother, the Yale freshman prince—were played and sung by Bonnie and me. And I, Emily, drifted around Manhattan casting spells to the tune of "Salagadoola menchicka boola bibbidi-bobbidi-boo."

Then there were the steppe sisters: Tevye's five daughters (which of them would marry first?) and Chekhov's *Three Sisters* (which of them endured the most ennui?). We longed to sneak into the Bijou to see a 1955 turkey called *Three Bad Sisters* (which of them was baddest?). A sororal trio was intriguing to us, who came in sets of two and four.

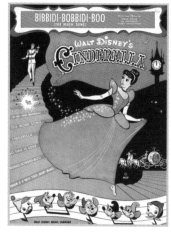

If two's company, wasn't three a crowd? Not for Faith, Hope, and Charity Cardwell of Sweetwater, Texas, the world's oldest triplets, who never lived more than twelve miles apart (Hope died last, at the age of ninety-seven, in 1997). But yes, it was a crowd for Elisabeth Kübler-Ross. Breaking away from her co-triplets, she left Switzerland to find singular prominence as the world-wide authority on compassionate death.

The Andrews and McGuire sisters weren't triplets, but they sang in three-part harmony—and we joined in. We were sister songbirds, and sister songbirds were in the air. The Pointers, the Roches, the McGarrigles, and the Calloways were still to come, but the oh-so-sweet Lennons were on TV, Patience and Prudence were on the radio, and the Simon sisters (before Carly shot out of the set to individual stardom) were down in the Village doing their folk-song act. Both of us were obsessed with Broadway show tunes, which we sang a cappella with our sisters. We were especially partial to "Ohio," the plaintive lament of the two frightened Sherwood girls in *Wonderful Town*.

Such devoted sisters were we that Bonnie and I, Ellen, made Irving Berlin's "Sisters" our theme song and

Introducing a quaint cavalcade of old-fashioned sisters . . .

...from vintage postcards...

inevitable encore after the Bach and Schubert piano-and-cello duets. Barbara and I, Emily, were enraptured by pictures in art books of beautiful sisters by Picasso, Gainsborough, and Rubens—but especially Renoir's *Two Girls at the Piano.* It showed a long-haired blonde playing, while a long-haired brunette stood behind her turning the pages. Since this is how we looked (after washing our hair with Ogilvie Sisters shampoo!) and how we arranged ourselves at the piano, we were sure it was us in a previous life.

We looked across the sea to Elizabeth and Margaret Rose, the young princesses at Buckingham Palace, and followed their royal progress in matching crowns and kilts while amusing ourselves at home with their paper-doll facsimiles. Further afield, we'd heard of the five British Mitford sisters and China's Soong

sisters (who married Chiang Kai-shek, Sun Yat-sen, and H. H. Kung) and discovered that Virginia Woolf not only had a room of her own but a sister named Vanessa Bell, too.

In the society pages, fashion and movie magazines, we read about sisterly lives of the rich and famous—the Kennedy girls (playing touch football with the boys at Hyannis Port), the Cushings (marrying their Roosevelts, Paleys, Whitneys, and Astors), and the beautiful Bennett sisters, Joan and Constance. At the Metropolitan Museum of Art in New York, we visited John Singer Sargent's majestic portrait of *The Wyndham Sisters* in their diaphanous gowns of white.

Now as then, famous or not, sisters in a set inhabit a concurrent landscape. Our intimacy profoundly affects the way we move, dress, flirt, cope, mourn, recover, even dream. Influenced by the order of our birth, we tend to fall into patterns, blending our maturing psyches into the family stew. In vying for approval and a slot in the family system, the balance of power is in constant flux. Who's older, who's smarter, who's prettier, who's more popular, who's made the better deal? Measuring sister against sister is an inevitable fact of life, both within the family and without.

At our best, we indulge each other's quirkiest habits and keep the darkest secrets, cross the country at a moment's notice to sit all night by a hospital bed or be a member of the wedding. We speak a form of shorthand using cryptic words, peculiar timbres, private signals. We can count on a dependable safety net in the world—although any safety net is only as dependable as its strongest strand. Sadly, and certainly, the sisterly bond can fray and even break. At our worst, we carry a grudge to the grave.

One of the most public sister splits—a spotlit display of rivalry—began about eighty years ago, minutes after Joan Fontaine became Olivia de Havilland's little sister. The de Havillands were born fifteen months

apart into a most peculiar household managed by an ambitious but spineless mother, an eccentric father, and, later, a brutal stepfather. Poised against this confusing backdrop were two antagonists with clashing temperaments: Olivia, cunning and her mother's favorite; Joan, moody and melancholy.

Neck and neck on the Hollywood track, they vied for love, vied for roles, vied for men, married and divorced almost simultaneously. In 1941, they even vied for Oscars (Joan won, for *Suspicion;* Olivia went on to win two of her own, for *To Each His Own* and *The Heiress*). The well-publicized feud continued throughout their careers, and even afterward. Olivia moved to Paris and wrote a book called *Every Frenchman Has One*. Joan stayed in the States and wrote a book called *No Bed of Roses.*

Joan Fontaine (left) and Olivia de Havilland in palmy days

Who was to blame for such a thorny sisterhood? Was it the press, who couldn't get enough of it? Was it the public, who lapped it up? Joan had the answer, which she spelled out in the final pages of her autobiography. It was Mommie Dearest.

In this epilogue, addressed to her late mother, she tried to comprehend the tension that had always existed between her and Olivia. "I never knew why you didn't try to make us kinder, more understanding, more forgiving of one another," she wrote in her long good-bye, "or did you prefer us at each other's throat?"

We ourselves prefer sisters at each other's side. "Sisters is probably *the* most competitive relationship within the family, but once the sisters are grown, it becomes the strongest relationship," observed Margaret Mead, the global anthropologist, about her sixty-eight-year relationship with her sister, Elizabeth. "On the whole, sisters would rather live with each other than anyone else in their old age."

The Delany sisters, Sadie (born in 1889) and Bessie (born in 1891), lived together for longer than any sisters we know of. Their father, born a slave on a Georgia plantation, was America's first Episcopal bishop. Their mother, one-eighth black and born free, taught them to stand tall and reach high. They did, from turn-of-the-century Raleigh to the *New York Times* bestseller list in the 1990s.

Ambitious and unafraid, they ventured north and arrived worlds ahead of their time. Together, they settled in Harlem and studied at Columbia. Sadie graduated and became the first black woman to teach home

Sadie (left) and Bessie Delany

economics in a New York City high school. "Dr. Bessie" graduated from the dental school and became the second black woman dentist ever to practice in New York State. Their careers mattered more than marriage, and they preferred each other's company above all.

And then one day in 1991, their long-term solitude was broken when a curious newspaper reporter came to call. The result: their picture in the paper, a 1993 best-seller called *Having Our Say*, an irresistible Broadway play based on it, and a thrilling rush of fame for two reclusive maiden ladies of a very certain age.

Suddenly the Delany sisters were stars. Their advice was solicited, their longevity admired. What was the recipe? Yoga, prayer, gardening, vitamins, cod-liver oil—and, as Bessie remarked, no husbands "to worry us to death." Plus, or even more important, their sisterness—a lifetime of mingled memories, shared pleasures, and an intimate understanding of just exactly what the other was thinking, feeling, needing.

"You can confide in a sister, share your secrets, and talk over your troubles with her," they wrote in their *Book of Everyday Wisdom*, published in 1994. "If you have a fuss, you have to make up. With a sister, you know it's forever."

The next year, forever came. At the age of 104, Bessie died in her sleep, and Sadie was, for the first time, on her own. Down but not out, she emerged from her grief with a third book. *On My Own at 107* was her tribute to and reflection on life without Bessie.

"Somewhere along the line I made up my mind I'm going to live, Bessie," she wrote. "I guess I probably don't have that much longer on this Earth, but I may as well make the best of it. Since the Lord has given me

...and snapshots and studio cards...

. . . and scrapbooks

this long life, the least I can do is be grateful. How can I give up on myself when the Lord hasn't?

"Bessie, I think I'm going to be all right."

~

It was high time we gathered our favorite sisters together in a book of our own. In attics and at tag sales, at flea markets and swap meets, we collected a quaint cavalcade of old-fashioned sisters on vintage postcards, studio cards, and snapshots. Two by two and three by three, together forever, we found Flossie and Myrtle in their white shirtwaists on the way to the textile mill, Mae and Margaret off to school with their lunch pails, and Lillie, Effie, and Ida smiling into the Pasadena sunshine. Some of the girls in this sepia series are dressed alike—in middie blouses, Buster Brown haircuts, white fur muffs, high-button shoes. The sisterness of others is more evident in the shape of a jaw, the turn of an ankle, or the earnestness with which they stare into the camera.

In *Twins on Twins,* a book by twin photographers Kathryn McLaughlin Abbe and Frances McLaughlin Gill, we fell upon a portrait of Maude and Michelle Bouvier, the twin aunts of Jacqueline and Lee Bouvier. Eager to reproduce the painting in our book, we placed a call to Maude's son, the writer John H. Davis. He couldn't deliver a color print of the painting, but he did deliver much more.

"Wouldn't you like to see the picture in person?" Mr. Davis asked, to our surprise and delight. "I think Mother would love to show it to you. Why don't I ask her?" And presto! Within a week, we were sipping tea on Park Avenue with the enthusiastic ninety-one-year-old Maude Bouvier Davis as she sat beneath the very same Albert Herter portrait for which she and her sister had posed seventy years earlier (see page 34). Then she strode to a hall closet and took from its top shelf a prized possession: the book written by her two most famous nieces.

Jacqueline Bouvier and her younger sister, Lee, had kept a scrapbook-journal of their three-month trip abroad in the summer of 1951. They called it *One Special Summer*. With drawings and poems by Jackie, twenty-two, and handwritten narrative by Lee, eighteen, they described their days aboard the *Queen Elizabeth*, tooling around Europe in their Hillman Minx, meandering through London, Arles, Rome, the Pyrenees. They visited with Bernard Berenson and attended fancy-dress balls. In Paris, Jackie took sketching lessons; in Venice, Lee sang "Abadaba Honeymoon" in a futile audition for a singing teacher.

Years later, the long-forgotten album was discovered by their mother, Janet Auchincloss, for whom they'd created it. Lee led it to publication in 1974, with not a word or Steinbergian line changed. "We are not the Brontë sisters, but Jackie and I did occasionally put pen to paper," she modestly explained in her introduction.

Jacqueline Lee Bouvier Kennedy Onassis and Caroline Lee Bouvier Canfield Radziwill Ross played out the rest of their complex family history very much in public. When Jackie became first lady of the land and Lee her unofficial lady-in-waiting, the big-sister-little-sister relationship captured so tenderly in their joyous collaboration inevitably changed. The subsequent trips they took—as the guests of kings, prime ministers, and shipping magnates—were now public

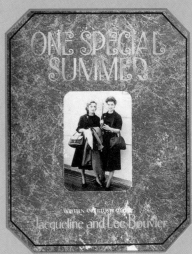

Top: *Maude Bouvier Davis at home in New York, sitting below the Herter portrait. She holds a photo commemorating her visit with Jackie at the White House.*
Above: *Her nieces' book*

property. Newspaper reporters were everywhere, tracking their travels.

"I can only look back on those trips and think how marvelous it would have been if we had recorded them as we had this first one," Lee wrote wistfully at the end of *One Special Summer*. "Perhaps we had lost some special sense of time, in growing up."

~

One day, while we were at our work station poring over an illustrated filmography of the Gish sisters (see page 55), we received a call from the New York Society Library, our home away from home. Would it be possible for Brooke Astor, a co-member, to borrow the very book we had borrowed? As an old friend of Lillian Gish, she had been asked to speak at an event celebrating the donation of the Lillian Gish Papers to the New York Public Library for the Performing Arts. With the intervention of the head librarian, the switch was made. When Mrs. Astor returned the book to us, she also sent along one perfect red rose. It was Valentine's Day, by chance, and we were charmed.

The Dionne Quintuplets, the quintessential sister set, lived in Canada and were years before our time (see page 80). But surfing the net, we soon learned that they had elicited the same frenzy in their day as Elvis and the Beatles did in ours. What's more, a fervent subculture still swirls around them. From club headquarters in Woburn, Massachusetts, comes the *Quint News* quarterly and a Quinvention once every five years. Devotees can savor old ads, bid on scrapbooks, swap teaspoons, or buy a white bib with pink trim actually worn by one of the quinfants.

Deep in Doublemint research, we were connected by the Wrigley Company to the original Doublemint Twins (see page 39). Joan and Jayne Boyd were alive and well and spending Thanksgiving together in Chicago. As a coda to our four-way telephone conversation, they doubled our pleasure with an impromptu rendition of the jingle they had made famous. They were also kind enough to send along an adorable picture of themselves as little girls in matching coats and bonnets.

Spinning the globe, we also found an assortment of geographical sisters. There was Sisters, Oregon, a sparkling town named for the Three Sisters mountains nearby. A legendary trio of waves called the Three Sisters used to lure sailors on Lake Michigan to their

Jayne and Joan Boyd in their Easter bonnets

Above: *The town founded by the Wells sisters*
Right: *The sisters Fox: Margaret and Kate*

watery graves, while the Three Sisters Islands poked their rocky heads out of the Potomac. And then there was Sistersville, West Virginia, where, in 1815, the two Wells sisters—Delilah and Sarah—turned their inheritance into a town.

Oh, how we yearned to go back in time to visit them all. . . .

Knock! knock! who's there? The sisters Fox, Margaret and Kate, who might have arranged the meeting. It's the sort of thing they did best. Perhaps.

It was a dark and stormy night in 1848 when the young girls first heard mysterious rappings in their Rochester farmhouse. In no time, they were holding séances in parlors and bringing word from loved ones who had crossed over. Poltergeists joined the party, tables floated, mirrors fell, and the "rapping" spree was in full force. Soon the gifted medium sisters were basking in an aura of their own, supported by intellectuals and politicians, praised by James Fenimore Cooper,

touted by Horace Greeley in the *New York Tribune*, and put on exhibition by their entreprenurial older sister.

Theirs was a long run. As pioneers on the psychic path, their magnetism attracted followers and skeptics and radiated out to other cities and other lands. Never mind that their mystical triumphs turned out to be a hoax, that their meteoric rise eventually sent them crashing. The Fox sisters helped popularize spiritualism, and they had a good time doing it for close to fifty years.

In putting sister after sister on our pages, we have had a good time, too.

～

One

FABLED SISTERS

✳ ✳ ✳ ✳ ✳ ✳ ✳ ✳ ✳ ✳ ✳ ✳ ✳ ✳ ✳ ✳ ✳ ✳ ✳ ✳

The magnetic power of sisters together—standing tall, snuggling close, in harmony or rivalry—has been an irresistible pull through the pages of time. From the very beginning, sister stories have been told of heavenly stars and woodland nymphs, goddesses of remarkable beauty and princesses who cast enchanted spells, sisters who wandered the desert, inspired symphonies, and stirred up trouble at the cauldron.

The first documented sister set was created by the mating of Mother Earth and Father Sky. These mythological giantesses, the Titanesses, were female counterparts to their brothers, the Titans. They all wed one another and began to beget. Titan Cronus and Titaness Rhea begat Zeus, the king of the gods.

A celestial cluster sparkles in the night sky of early spring. These are the seven Pleiades, and the story of their ascension is woven with melodrama and magic. Once upon an ancient Grecian afternoon, these alluring nymphs were to be found gamboling in a sylvan glen. Orion, the handsome hunter, found them and was bedazzled. He pursued the sisters relentlessly, and they begged Zeus for help. The king of the gods remodeled them into doves and cast them heavenward.

In the fifty million years since their rise to glory in the constellation Taurus, the seven starry sisters have attained a position of intellectual prominence on earth as it is in heaven. Sister-minded Sappho sang of them, as did Benjamin Britten and Homer. Tennyson poeticized them as "a swarm of fireflies tangled in a silver braid." The Seven Sisters still symbolize feminine powers of strength and wisdom, as evidenced by the "Seven Sisters" on the New England college circuit and the "Seven Sisters" on the women's magazine stand.

The Pleiades had a flock of seven half sisters, the Hyades, who lived nearby in Taurus. They arrived there fraught with sadness. Their mother had been killed by a wild animal, and the girls were stranded. The ubiquitously attentive Zeus rescued them from earthly danger and changed them into stars. For two billion years, these seven weepy sisters, still mourning the death of their mother, have appeared in the sky to portend the rainy season.

Wafting through the mythical halls of Mount Olympus, the nine Muses were helping in other ways. As the first significant female patrons of the arts, the violet-wreathed sisters began their careers inspiring men—perching on a sculptor's shoulder, whispering in a poet's ear, plucking a composer's lyre. Such was their devotion to culture that their very name became rooted in such words as music, museum, and amusement.

"He is happy whom the Muses love," Hesiod noticed. And successful, too. Each sister had her own niche in the world of arts and crafts. Calliope, for example, presided over epic poetry. Clio guided mapmakers and historians—and also found time to invent the lute. Melpomene held the mask of tragedy and prompted such brooding dramatists as Aeschylus, Strindberg, and O'Neill. Thalia, on the other hand, held the mask of comedy for Charlie Chaplin and Groucho Marx. Erato hosted marriage feasts and uttered love poems. Terpsichore propelled the choreog-

The nine Muses dance around a colleague from Olympus.

raphy of Martha Graham and Fred Astaire. Polyhymnia handled hymns. Euterpe created the chorus and sparked the passions of Bach, Beethoven, and Andrew Lloyd Webber. The globe-toting Urania, named for her great-grandfather Uranus, stimulated the study of astronomy.

Elsewhere in the neighborhood were the three Graces (also known as the three Charities) named Aglaia, Euphrosyne, and Thalia. While these blithe spirits were busy bestowing beauty, tenderness, harmony, cheerfulness, and sensuality, other sister sets were focusing on the environment. The Horae, goddesses of the seasons, oversaw the colorful transition from the whites of winter to the pastels of spring. The Hesperides hovered over the orchards of the gods, taking a particular interest in guarding the golden apples. Drifting through shady groves were the Heliades, who celebrated the poplar tree, and the Dryads, who glorified the oak. The nearby Naiads took responsibility for brooks, springs, fountains, and wells. By the mythological sea, sisterly schools of aquatic nymphs—the Oceanides and the Nereides—rode dolphins, carried tridents, and trailed garlands of flowers through the waves.

But not all legendary sister sets were goody-goodies. Myth reverberates with chilling images of terrible trios and bad hair days. Among the first, and worst, were the Gorgons with their coifs of hissing snakes, their scaly bodies, brass hands, and tusk-like teeth. So hideous were they that anyone who looked upon them was turned to stone. Not Perseus, however. He killed the baddest-seed sister, Medusa, and went off with her head as a souvenir. Soon, due to the remarkable bravery of this feat, small replicas were being sold in the agora as lucky charms.

The Heliades (tree nymphs), from a 1499 woodcut by Francesco Colonna

Even more hideous than the Gorgon girls were the Harpies. Sisterly monsters with steely feathers and slashing claws, they lived in filth, spread disease, and snatched the souls of the dead. Their cousins, the three man-hating Furies with their black-dog faces and bat wings, crouched together at the entrance to Hades. As the personification of rage and slaughter, they punished those who sinned against women. "I acknowledge the Furies, I believe in them, I have heard the disastrous beating of their wings," quaked American novelist Theodore Dreiser as late as 1911, proving that the sisters' negative vibes were by no means limited to the land of the gods.

The three Fates had more cosmic chores. From cradle to grave, one of the mythological sisters either attended every birth, spun the thread of life, or cut it. Shakespeare paid them homage when he recast them as the three witches in *Macbeth*, gathered around the cauldron.

Cinderellas BY THE SCORE

No accounting of sibling rivalry and revelry spins so gossamer a web of enchantment—nor enjoys a wider fame among young and old—than the story of poor, put-upon Cinderella. Charles Perrault's original story, itself spun from elements in French and Italian folk legend, appeared in 1697; not long thereafter it gained recognition as a charming subject for opera.

Think of the potential: the contrasts between the sweet, lyrical heroine and her nattering, preening sisters; the fine chance for a blustery comic monologue or two by the ill-tempered stepparent (*father* in Perrault's original tale, mother in some later versions). One point worth noting: The famous glass slipper—which, as any shoe salesman will tell you, makes for impractical footwear on the ballroom floor or anywhere else—came about through a mistranslation in Perrault's manuscript; his slipper of *vair* ("fur") somehow ended up as *verre* ("glass").

The first Cinderella opera to survive was the *Cendrillon* of Jean-Louis de Larouette, which had a brief run in Paris in 1759; half a century later a second setting, by the Maltese composer Nicolò Isouard, fared somewhat better. Both were soon blown away, however, by the marvelous *La Cenerentola* by the twenty-five-year-old Gioacchino Rossini, immediately recognized as a comic masterpiece when first performed in 1817.

Jacopo Ferretti's text makes some interesting departures from Perrault, mostly at the request of Rossini, who tended to quail before the specter of the Italian censor; thus, the notorious slipper, which might have ordained an onstage display of raw ankle, became a bracelet. Rossini also had little patience with the supernatural elements; rather than the fairy godmother and her pumpkin coach, Cenerentola comes to the ball with the help of two of the prince's flunkies. No matter. She beats out her wretched stepsisters in the inevitable any-note-you-can-sing-I-can-sing-higher confrontation, gets her prince, and displays both voice and virtue by forgiving all her evildoers at the end.

Disregarding the gory retelling by the Brothers Grimm, Jules Massenet stuck to Perrault's gossamer-light, sugary-sweet setting for *Cendrillon*, his 1899 opera. His music, with its echoes of a bygone style, whispers and tinkles and charms the senses; he compounds the otherworldliness by setting the Prince's music for a mezzo-soprano.

Sergei Prokofiev's ravishing, evening-length *Cinderella* ballet from 1944 remains in the repertories of both Russia's Kirov and Britain's Royal ballets. Composed in the Soviet Union's darkest wartime years, it also returns to the Perrault tale for its inspiration. So, you might say, does Walt Disney's animated version of 1950, which, in true Disney fashion, presents Cinderella with a pair of singing mice for companionship. But any movie that enriches the world's fund of popular song with "Bibbidi-Bobbidi-Boo" can't be all bad.

‿ Alan Rich, music critic,
L.A. Weekly

Double double was the trouble in the land of Canaan. Lot and his two daughters appeared in the first recorded tale of incest (Genesis 19). Jacob, Leah, and Rachel starred in the first published romance of one man involved with two sisters—both of whom he married, the eldest first (Genesis 29). Later, over in the New Testament, Mary and Martha entered into the first recorded sisterly clash (Luke 10).

From the mist of ancient myth and the dust of the biblical desert, legendary sister sets traveled on to the fairy-tale kingdom. They progressed from drifting through sacred groves to waltzing in mirrored halls. And the significance of birth order went along, too.

"The Twelve Dancing Princesses," produced by the Brothers Grimm, slept together in twelve beds all in a row. Every night their father locked them in their room. But somehow, every night the princesses managed to escape, traveled through a diamond forest to a splendid ballroom, and danced the night away—as well as the soles of their shoes. A soldier, poor but honest, solved the mystery of their disappearing act. As a reward, he was allowed to marry the oldest—attended by her eleven sisters as bridesmaids—and lived happily ever after, on his father-in-law's throne.

Elsewhere in the enchanted forest of fairyland, "Snow White and Rose Red" took life more seriously. Both girls were lovely and kind, to each other and to their beloved mother. Opposites by nature—one lively and outgoing, the other quiet and thoughtful—they let no harsh word or mean thought ever escape their lips. Because of their harmonious relationship, they represented the idealization of sisterhood. When they rescued a bear bewitched by an evil dwarf who turned out to be a handsome and wealthy prince, there was no problem of sibling rivalry. Snow White married him, and Rose Red settled down with his brother. And Mother got her own room at the Palace.

The quintessential story of sibling rivalry and the most popular of all fairy tales is "Cinderella." This timeless tale of three sisters, one good as gold and the other two crazed with envy, is so pertinent to the ongoing family drama that it has been told and retold through the centuries. Along with Prokofiev, Massenet, Rossini, and Disney, there is Ferenc Molnar's *The Glass Slipper* on stage, Leslie Caron's *Glass Slipper* on screen, Rodgers and Hammerstein's *Cinderella* on television, Jerry Lewis's *Cinderfella* on tape—with no end in sight.

⌁

From a bitter hearth in fairyland to a small village in rural England, many a literary sister was under pressure to find her man. In the early nineteenth century, Jane Austen was the preeminent chronicler of a particular social scene in which Prince Charming no longer had a crown and castle but rather money, rank, and a splendid country estate. She satirized this mannered and regulated world through her stories about sisters who knew their place in the pecking order as well as in local society. Whether they were taking long, talky walks together, sitting demurely in the parlor, or acting giddy and gossipy at the balls to which they were always invited, their main concern in life was who would marry first.

Actually, Jane Austen herself chose to watch from the wings, comment ironically, and never marry. Her closest friendship was with her beloved older sister, Cassandra, whom she certainly used as a model for one or another of her characters. "If Cassandra were going

*Snow White
and Rose Red
at the garden gate*

to have her head cut off," their mother observed of her younger daughter's adulation, "Jane would insist on sharing her fate."

The Dashwood sisters in Austen's *Sense and Sensibility* were just as devoted to each other. She began her Sussex-based satire as a novel-in-letters, calling it *Elinor and Marianne* for the two main characters she had fashioned after Cassandra and herself. Reworked as a straightforward narrative, the book was published in 1811—credited only to "A Lady" on the title page—and has remained in print ever since. The versatile British actress Emma Thompson adapted the novel for the screen in 1995 and starred in it herself, playing Elinor, the sensible one.

In *Pride and Prejudice,* there were five Bennet sisters to marry off, ideally in chronological order. Once again, the two main characters—Jane, the eldest, and Elizabeth, the most intriguing—were based on Cassandra and Jane Austen. Mrs. Bennet, the manipulative mother of this nubile brood, was a superficial and silly creature, solely devoted to the matrimonial task. But while her sisters understood their role in the social scheme, Elizabeth refused. Such a rebel daughter, who would rather marry for love than for money, was perhaps too intelligent and surely way ahead of her time. Despite her resistance, she managed to marry for love *and* money.

In the nearly two hundred years since its publication, *Pride and Prejudice* has inspired myriad versions and accumulated a strangely eclectic cast of cobblers from the 1940 Hollywood take by Aldous Huxley to the 1959 Broadway musical flop by Abe Burrows to the 1995 television miniseries produced by the BBC.

Out on the moody moors of Yorkshire, where there were no cotillions, no tea parties, and no landed gentry to land, the Brontë sisters—Charlotte, Emily,

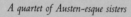
A quartet of Austen-esque sisters

and Anne—were compelled to come up with their own entertainment. Isolated though they were at Haworth Parsonage with their widowed father, the girls and their brother, Branwell, were brilliantly aware of the nineteenth-century world outside.

The Reverend Mr. Brontë subscribed to the major periodicals of the day, and his children eagerly absorbed all they could. They constructed plays, wrote poems, painted pictures, and produced miniature books about imaginary kingdoms named Gondal and Angria. Thus did they weave what Charlotte called a "web of sunny air" to divert them from their sadness. (Just beyond the front door was the family graveyard where their young mother and two sisters lay.)

In 1846, the Brontës became a published sister set—pseudonymously. Their first professional collaboration, a book of poems, was credited to Currer (Charlotte), Ellis (Emily), and Acton (Anne) Bell

"because," explained Charlotte several years later, "without at that time suspecting that our mode of writing and thinking was not what is called 'feminine'—we had a vague impression that authoresses are liable to be looked on with prejudice." While this volume was being critically applauded but commercially ignored (two copies out of one thousand were sold), the undaunted threesome continued to write away.

Within the next two years, they were rewarded with the publication of Emily's *Wuthering Heights*, Anne's *Agnes Grey*, and Charlotte's *Jane Eyre*—again under masculine pen names. It was not until after their deaths, in the middle of the nineteenth century, in fact, that their true identities were ever revealed to the public.

By 1900, their actual names were very well known indeed and their fame widespread. American novelist William Dean Howells wrote to his sister about the Brontës' powerful pull. "Have you ever read *Wuthering*

Greer Garson and her sisters in the 1940 Pride and Prejudice

Heights? It is a prodigious book. It is wonderful how those girls turned themselves loose. *Jane Eyre* would startle people nowadays by its boldness."

Charlotte outlived her siblings and mourned them for the rest of her life. "I am free to walk on the moors," she wrote, "but when I go out there alone everything reminds me of the times when others were with me, and then the moors seem a wilderness, featureless, solitary, saddening. My sister Emily had a particular love for them, and there is not a knoll of heather, nor a branch of fern, nor a young bilberry leaf or linnet, but reminds me of her. The distant prospects were Anne's delight, and when I look round she is in the blue tints, the pale mists, the waves and shadows of the horizon."

The emotional undercurrents of the Brontës' fiction were made for Hollywood. Charlotte's *Jane Eyre* has been filmed more than a dozen times, beginning with two silents in 1910. But the most famous Jane was surely Joan Fontaine, who starred in the 1944 film as the beleaguered governess in love with Orson Welles (and who, as a girl at the Lowood School, meets up with a young and poignant Elizabeth Taylor in a cameo role).

Emily's indelibly dark *Wuthering Heights* has been filmed over and over again, even in French and Spanish. None of the productions, however, can hold even a flickering candle to the unforgettable 1939 version. The on-screen passion of Merle Oberon as Cathy and Laurence Olivier as the obsessive, smoldering Heathcliff was contagious. Every sister yearned for a Heathcliff of her own, a lover who would pursue her through mist and moor to the end of time.

~

From nineteenth-century England to nineteenth-century New England. Enter *Little Women*, the classic American novel immortalizing the penniless March sisters of Concord, Massachusetts. The story has been cherished for over a century because it resonates with family life as it's truly lived—or as one would long for it to be. Ironically, Louisa May Alcott wrote her masterpiece more to satisfy her publisher's request for "a girls' story" than to please herself.

"I begin *Little Women*," she complained to her journal in May 1868. "I plod away, though I don't enjoy this sort of thing. Never liked girls or knew many, except my sisters; but our queer plays and experiences may prove interesting, though I doubt it."

Louisa May used her sisters—and their special interests—as prototypes for her characters. Anna Alcott, the oldest, loved theater and belonged to the Concord Dramatic Union; she became Meg. Elizabeth, the shy musician, died of scarlet fever at twenty-two; she was Beth. May, the artist, studied with William Morris Hunt at the School of Design in Boston and

EVERYBODY LOVES

LITTLE WOMEN

M-G-M's NEW
COLOR BY
TECHNICOLOR
ROMANCE!

Starring

JUNE ALLYSON · PETER LAWFORD
MARGARET O'BRIEN · ELIZABETH TAYLOR
JANET LEIGH · ROSSANO BRAZZI · MARY ASTOR
WITH LUCILE WATSON · SIR C. AUBREY SMITH · HARRY DAVENPORT
A MERVYN LeROY PRODUCTION
SCREEN PLAY BY ANDREW SOLT, SARAH Y. MASON AND VICTOR HEERMAN · FROM THE NOVEL BY LOUISA MAY ALCOTT
PRODUCED AND DIRECTED BY MERVYN LeROY · A METRO-GOLDWYN-MAYER PICTURE

The March girls go to Hollywood.
Right: Winona Ryder and her sisters do good in the 1994 version.

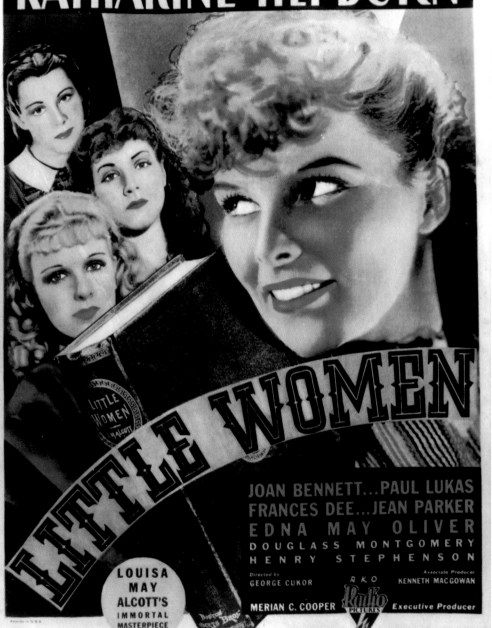

became a renowned watercolorist; she was Amy. And Louisa, the writer, was fictionalized as Jo, the writer.

The plight of poverty seems almost to nurture a special kind of sororal bonding in popular fiction. The story of the four March girls and their home filled with love, if not possessions, is so resonant that it has reached the screen in at least three versions. Hollywood's Jo was played by the feisty Katharine Hepburn in the well-loved 1933 rendition, the freckly June Allyson in the treacly one of 1949, and the winsome Winona Ryder in 1994. The four March sisters also inspired a set of greeting cards made by Hallmark in the 1950s and an exquisite quartet of dolls made by Madame Alexander (who was herself the oldest of four sisters).

In the storied world of sisters, dozens more landed in New York. The Blythe Girls—Helen, Margy, and Rose—inhabited a series of juvenile books by Laura Lee Hope that were published in the twenties. The poor-and-Pollyannaish trio shared a flat in Manhattan, supporting one another in their sisterly search for love and adventure. Elsewhere in the great metropolis, the five sisters in Sydney Taylor's *All-of-a-Kind Family* were growing up on the Lower East Side. The beloved series of children's books, published in the 1950s and 1960s, grew out of Taylor's own childhood as one of five sisters.

Down in Greenwich Village, homesick and hud-dled together in their basement flat, were two career girls from out of town. The Sherwood sisters—Ruth, the writer, and Eileen, the actress—entered laughing in Ruth McKenney's semi-autobiographical stories. First published by *The New Yorker* in the thirties and then collected into a book called *My Sister Eileen,* the sisters' salad days were tossed on stage as a 1940 Broadway play with Shirley Booth and Jo Ann Sayers. Thence followed a 1942 movie with Rosalind Russell and Janet Blair as

the small-town sisters, a lackluster 1955 movie musical with Betty Garrett and Janet Leigh, and a short-lived 1960 television series with Elaine Stritch and Shirley Bonne.

The only version not called *My Sister Eileen*—and surely the best version—was the 1953 Broadway musical *Wonderful Town* starring Rosalind Russell (once again) and Edith Adams. Why, o why, o why o the girls ever left Ohio was to find fame and fortune in the big city. After contending with assorted wolves, jackals, agents, editors, landlords, Brazilian sailors, and Irish cops, they did.

Nothing gives the playwright more to play with than a tangled, tortured trio of sisters. Consider Anton Chekhov's *Three Sisters,* which opened in Moscow in 1900. Although the compelling Masha, Olga, and Irina longed to leave the Russian provinces for the big city, it was not to be. Restless at home, doomed only to dream, the Prozorov girls yearned to escape their disintegrating

*Mia Farrow, Barbara Hershey, and
Dianne Wiest as Woody Allen's troubled trio*

world. The story's emotional impact is very real and very playable, with three juicy female roles.

Unlike the melancholy Russians who stayed at home and clung to each other, Wendy Wasserstein's three *Sisters Rosenzweig* set out just as soon as they could. Off they went to three separate continents. Not so Woody Allen's metropolitan threesome. Lovingly neurotic, *Hannah and Her Sisters* fulfilled a secret but prevalent male fantasy: If one sister is good, two are better. There are no boundaries, in movieland at least, when it's all in the family. And it's certainly all in the family with the Ephron sisters, Nora and Delia, who work together on witty and wonderful movies such as *This Is My Life* and *Michael*, writing and directing side by side.

The Hallmark set of Little Women *dolls, based on the 1949 movie*

27

Two

DOUBLE TAKE

Young or old, modest or vain, there is no escaping the primal fascination with the reflected self, whether that reflected self is seen in a pool, glass window, or boudoir mirror. Then it's a small leap, and an irresistible one, to look beyond the looking glass—to see double in the outside world.

Having a twin is a dream come true, the actual representation of a universal fantasy. As a twin and her twin stroll together down the avenue, pose primly for a portraitist, turn a cartwheel in unison, or dispense parallel advice to the lovelorn, they comprise a charismatic unit. Together they dwell in a mystical place, radiate a certain magic, know things others can't know. As twinness spins its special thread, weaving extrasensory moments and odd intertwinings, its uniqueness drifts through legend and sparks superstition.

The first twins appeared as a complex mythological quartet. The lovely Leda was already pregnant by Tyndareus, king of Sparta, when she was seduced by Zeus, king of the gods, in the guise of a swan. In due time, she gave birth simultaneously to not one, but two pairs of twins. One boy-and-girl set, the children of her mortal husband, were Clytemnestra and Castor. The other twins, Helen and Pollux, were the children of Zeus.

All four offspring went on to fame and glory: Castor and Pollux changed birth partners and teamed up to inspire the constellation Gemini. As for the girls, Helen and Clytemnestra were the first twin sisters in recorded history—and the archetypes of good twin–bad twin. The beautiful Helen became queen of Sparta, the inamorata of Paris, and the catalyst for the Trojan War. The devious

Opposite: *Twin nuns at Cape May, New Jersey*

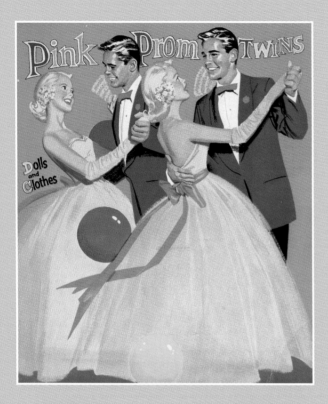

A GIRL SO FAIR, I THOUGHT THAT THERE
COULD BE NONE TO EQUAL THE CREATURE—
BUT WHEN I SAW HER SISTER TWIN,
I SAID,"HERE'S A REAL DOUBLE FEATURE."

Clytemnestra killed her husband, Agamemnon, and her husband's lover, Cassandra, and was then herself killed by her son, Orestes.

Mothers residing on earth can expect less input from the gods and more from science. "In the United States today, at least eleven births out of every thousand are twins, which is to say that about one person in fifty has a twin (about one-third of these are identical). That constitutes a virtual epidemic," according to Lawrence Wright's 1995 article on twinning in *The New Yorker*. "Between 1973 and 1990, twin births shot up at twice the rate of singletons, and triplets and higher multiple-births increased at seven times the single-birth rate—partly because many women are waiting until later in life to have children, and multiple births are more frequent among older mothers." And partly because of fertility drugs. "Now," adds Dr. Louis Keith, the president of the Center for the Study of Multiple Births, "doctors are prescribing ovulation-enhancing agents as if they were prescribing bubble gum at a children's birthday party."

Biologically, there are two kinds of twins: identical and fraternal. When a single egg fertilized by one sperm splits in half, and each half becomes a fetus, the result is identical twins: matching children of the same gender with the same genes. When two eggs are released simultaneously and fertilized by two sperms, the two fetuses develop into fraternal twins: two boys, two girls, or one of each—unmatching, genetically different, two siblings who happened to share a womb.

Unlike other siblings who must be taught to share, twins are born having to. From the get-go—mother's milk, father's time, the playpen, the pram—it's share and share alike. Their possessions—a "lefty"

Abigail Van Buren (left) and Ann Landers back in Sioux City, Iowa, to attend their 50th high school reunion

or "righty" spoon, a blue or yellow bike—become the things that define them. Because they arrive and mature simultaneously, they use two of everything at the same time: two forks, two toothbrushes, two dolls, two boxes of crayons, two mouthfuls of braces.

But one party. "When my friends threw me a bridal shower, and I saw the balloons and streamers, I burst into tears," says Monica Leaf, a twin from Rittenhouse Square. "I realized that it was the first time in my whole life there'd ever been a party that was for me alone. Just me."

As if life weren't confusing enough, well-meaning parents may perpetuate an already tricky situation. "Twins have an even harder time trying to grow up as the two distinct young people they really are," advises a 1959 manual called *How to Help Your Children.* "Parents can help if they don't assume that because twins are identical or almost identical in looks, they necessarily want to dress alike, to do the same thing at the same

time, or always like the same activities and the same friends."

Many twins, however, delight in their alikeness. The Friedman sisters of Sioux City, Iowa, entered the world seventeen minutes apart on July 4, 1918. Not only were they identical twins; they were even named to reflect their mirror image: Pauline Esther and Esther Pauline. Popo and Eppie were good talkers, good listeners, and, in college, good enough writers to collaborate on a gossip column called "The Campus Rat." Two days before their twenty-first birthday, they became two on the aisle when they were married in a spectacular double wedding.

But surely they are best known for their parallel careers. For some forty years, they have enjoyed double exposure, each twin's photo appearing with her own wildly popular syndicated newspaper column. Today, the Friedman twins are known as Dear Abby and Ann Landers.

Harriet and Eliza Stowe in an 1855 daguerreotype

"I took the 'Abigail' from the Old Testament, for Abigail was a prophetess in the Book of Samuel, and it was said of her, 'Blessed art thou, and blessed is thy advice, O Abigail,'" explained the former Pauline Esther in *The Best of Dear Abby,* her 1981 book. "For my last name I chose 'Van Buren' from our eighth president, Martin Van Buren, because I liked the aristocratic, old-family ring."

The original Ann Landers was actually a nurse with an advice column in the Chicago *Sun-Times.* When she died in 1955, the column was up for grabs. Eppie competed for it and won the byline. Now she owns it.

For two sisters dispensing advice about love and family relationships, these two are curiously at odds. But perhaps their rivalry for readers, their refusal to discuss each other in print, and their on-again, off-again association is their way of separating and declaring their independence from the vicissitudes of twin life.

⁓

Some twins remain each other's fondest home companion. Such was the choice of Harriet Beecher Stowe's twin daughters, who were glad to tend the hearth. The most famous of Stowe's thirty-two works of fiction, *Uncle Tom's Cabin,* set the world on fire in 1852. The dark-eyed Hattie and Eliza, on the other hand, did nothing of the kind.

Their birth, on the evening of September 29, 1836, was, as such things often were in those days, a complete surprise to the parties involved. As their famous minister uncle, Henry Ward Beecher, wrote to relatives: "Harriet has got along bravely—& is quite forward after such a singular exploit, or rather I should have called a plural one." More than that, the exhausted, overworked Harriet was rapturous. She wrote to a friend that "tho I scarcely slept a wink last night & tho I have had one of two babies in my arms all day—tho money is scarce & times hard yet I never was happier on the whole than I am now."

As New England girls coming of age, the twins attended the Abbot Academy in Andover. They traveled abroad, studying foreign languages, visiting art galleries, buying French finery, and attending their very first opera. But their austere clergyman father, disturbed by their new sophistication, made it clear that he required their presence at home. From then on, the girls obeyed, becoming a versatile management team. They ran the household (which included two homes and four younger children) and, as proofreaders and graceful correspondents, were invaluable to their parents' careers.

The twins—"lively, vivacious, with a real genius for practical life" (as their mother put it)—certainly must have experienced affairs of the heart and other emotional upheavals. But their primary attachment was to each other. They never married, remaining at Nook Farm, the Stowe family home in Hartford, until death (in their seventies) did them part.

A daguerreotype taken at nineteen remains their most enduring legacy. Within a graceful frame, the twins pose demurely in off-the-shoulder dresses of matching taffeta, matching chokers and bracelets. Their smooth dark hair, parted severely in the middle, falls into fashionable corkscrew curls. Although they wear identical outfits, they wear unidentical expressions. Harriet seems haunted and serious, her gloved hands clasping a folding fan on her lap. Eliza, almost smiling, rests her chin pensively on her hand.

~

Matching sisters in matching attire have long been the artist's muse. The divine times two. "What a challenge to paint twins!" note twin authors Kathryn McLaughlin Abbe and Frances McLaughlin Gill in *Twins on Twins.* "The artist does not simply paint one person twice. Rather, he must record each of the twins as individuals; must be aware of subtle differences between the two in such things as hand gesture, tilt of the head, and the look in the eye, whether a direct gaze or a downward or sideward glance. The true artist notices these differences quickly, and delights in his sensitive observations."

One of the most impressive paintings of twin sisters, and one that does take in their subtle differences, is Albert Herter's profile portrait of the Bouvier twins. In the 1920s, the colorful comings and goings of Maude and Michelle were followed avidly—by photographers, social arbiters, and society editors (although not quite so avidly, perhaps, as the comings and goings of their nieces, Jacqueline and Lee Bouvier, some thirty years later).

The twins arrived ten minutes apart on a hot summer day in 1905 to the astonishment of their parents, Mr. and Mrs. John V. Bouvier, Jr. "Mother and Father were married sixteen years when we were born," says Maude today, sipping a proper cup of tea in her Park Avenue apartment. "We had brother Jack—Jackie's father—and another brother, Bud, and sister

Maude and Michelle Bouvier with friend in East Hampton

Michelle and Maude Bouvier in Albert Hecter's portrait

Edith. Father was so put out! Twins! And red hair! The others were all dark, you know."

They burst into this well-established household, taking over the boys' room as their nursery and virtually eclipsing their older sister. "With their long red curls, freckled noses, their cheerful voices, their merry ways, they attracted the major share of attention," wrote Maude's son, John H. Davis, in his 1969 saga of *The Bouviers*. More than that, "they became something of a cult in the family, a double deity against whose sacred status their brothers and sister would compete in vain."

The twins epitomized an enchanted moment in New York society. They studied at Spence and Miss Porter's, summered in East Hampton, picnicked on velvet lawns, won Charleston contests, were launched at Sherry's, and performed on command. "We never had a singing lesson or played the piano," Maude recalls, "but we used to go to these things—at the Plaza, the Park Lane, the Ritz Ballroom—and sing in close harmony."

For their sixteenth birthday, they were given a black flivver, which they shared. Otherwise, they were given double everything. And when they weren't, it rankled. "Santa Claus gave me a doll once that was larger than my twin's doll," remembers Maude, vividly. "But I didn't *want* anything different."

The twins were inseparable and each other's best friend though they were quite different in temperament. "I was positive, practical, not a worrier. I always adjusted to what was going on. Michelle was negative, high-strung, a real worrywart. She was very effervescent, and I was more the quiet one. But she was very delicate, like a beautiful flower. She married young, and she was homesick on her honeymoon."

Always they dressed alike—"We never thought *not* to dress alike"—in frocks handmade by their dressmaker. Their mother, who bought the fabrics at Lord & Taylor, preferred that they wear greens and browns, with bronze party shoes. "A lot of brown," remembers Maude, "with brown satin hair ribbons only. Mother was artistic and played up the red hair."

In the Herter painting, they're twenty-one and pretty in pink—wearing dresses "bought off the rack." Michelle, newly married, is on the left, wearing a long taffeta creation by Lanvin. Maude's, decorated with crystal beads, began flapperishly short, but she asked the artist to lengthen it for the formal portrait. The 1926 painting is a poignant study of twinness, pastel and pensive, and it indelibly captures Maude and Michelle in bloom.

⁓

Orbiting the same world at the same time, but on a faster track, were Gloria and Thelma, "The Miraculous Morgans" and sometimes "The Magical Morgans" or "The Magnificent Morgans"—thus designated by New York's worshipful gossip columnist, Cholly Knickerbocker. Sir Cecil Beaton, another devotee, described the identical twins as: "Alike as two magnolias, with raven tresses, flowing dresses, slight lisps and foreign accents." They "diffuse an atmosphere of hot-house elegance and lacy femininity."

Unrelated to J. Pierpont Morgan (but in no rush to disenchant those who thought they were), the girls were born in 1906, the daughters of Harry Hays Morgan, a career diplomat, and his volatile wife, Laura. Life was mostly abroad, languages were entirely foreign; the girls didn't speak English until they were eleven.

When they returned to the States, they took a bachelorette flat in Greenwich Village and bedazzled the town. In 1923, "Glorious Gloria" married Reginald Claypole Vanderbilt, who had graduated from Yale into a sporty New York life. Promptly, they produced a baby daughter. But alas, within months, champagne-soaked Reggie was dead, leaving Big Gloria with Little Gloria and Little Gloria with $6 million.

Meanwhile, Thelma was sowing some aristocratic oats abroad. She had married the hot-tempered Lord Furness, heir to the British steamship lines, but was in love with the Prince of Wales. Weekends were spent with him at Fort Belvedere. "He puttered in the garden, pruned his trees, blew on his bagpipes," she remembered in the dual autobiography she wrote with her twin. "I was sublimely happy; the comfortable simplicity was all that I wanted, and I was pleased that we were spared the *Sturm und Drang* that is the traditional background of a love such as ours." Little did she dream of the *Sturm und Drang* to come.

In New York, her twin sister was embroiled in something far less picturesque. Hard-pressed to take on the responsibilities of motherhood, Gloria would often leave town—and leave her young daughter in hired hands. Such behavior did nothing to endear her to her austere sister-in-law, Gertrude Vanderbilt Whitney, nor to her own mother. As a result, the most famous and closely watched custody battle of the century exploded in 1934—pitting mother Gloria against aunt Gertrude over Little Gloria.

Thelma was needed at her sister's side, and the royal idyll couldn't last. Before leaving England, Thelma made certain provisions to keep the prince

*"The Magnificent Morgans": Gloria (left)
and Thelma aboard the* Normandie *in 1937*

from missing her too much. She enlisted the aid of her new best friend, Wallis Simpson, an already-twice-divorced Baltimore belle.

"Oh, Thelma, the little man is going to be so lonely," Mrs. Simpson sympathized.

"Well, dear," Thelma suggested, "you look after him for me while I'm away. See that he does not get into any mischief."

So Wallis did what any good friend would do. She filled the prince's dance card, she filled his life, and she married him.

Gloria lost her daughter. Thelma lost her prince. But the twin bond remained tight. "Thank God my mother had Thelma, because they really were like a mirror image of each other," recalled Little Gloria Vanderbilt many years later, "and not only that, but so supportive of each other. It was as if my mother and Thelma were married. When you think of it, imagine, from birth, being in a room with someone who looks exactly like you and is just there as an extension of yourself."

~

"Which Twin has the Toni?" This was the question on everyone's lips in the forties and fifties. The ad's message was that the difference was indiscernible between a $2 Toni home permanent and the more expensive version done at Cora's Salon de Beauté.

"Understandably, the initial reaction of the beauty shop operator to the home permanent was violent," recalled ad man Fairfax M. Cone years later. "The makers of Toni were accused of fakery and fraud; and it was whispered in loud stage whispers that a Toni home permanent was the first step toward feminine baldness. Beauticians ran joint advertisements in newspapers and filled their windows with posters attacking the home permanent, even to the point of saying that they would not be responsible for the result of any later treatment of home-waved hair."

"Calling all Twins!" cried an ad of 1949. Eager to trade their straight hair for curls and their anonymity for fame, America's twins responded. Winners of the Toni Twin Hunt would reap a double reward: their carefully coiffed tresses pictured in the pages of the country's leading women's magazines . . . and a free trip to South America! Toni Twins made public appearances from coast to coast, flouncing and primping and demonstrating their newly acquired skill with the home permanent technique at Macy's, Gimbel's, and other major department stores.

While the Toni girls were happily waving their hair in public, and the product was making headlines all over the country, other manufacturers were also twigging on to twins.

Wrigley's chewing gum—"double wrapped" with "double strength peppermint"—had been created in 1914. When *Double Everything*, a radio program sponsored by the company, premiered in 1938, it featured two comedians, two singers, two pianists, even two announcers.

From hearing double to seeing double, the promotional concept evolved under the aegis of Wrigley art director Otis Shepard. In 1939, the first twin beauties with matching teeth and hats beamed out from posters, billboards, bus and subway cards. Gum was good for you, they implied, and, indeed, it must have been. According to *The Psycho-Dynamics of Chewing*, published that same year by Dr. H. L. Hollingworth of Columbia University, chewing was said to relax tension and foster concentration.

In 1960, the drawings were shelved, and the Doublemint Twins came to life. Jayne and Joan Boyd, identical twin models from Hammond, Indiana, were

Otis Shepard's twins come to life as Jayne and Joan Boyd double our pleasure.

singing on a Chicago radio show when they were noticed by a scout in the control booth and introduced to none other than local gum king Philip W. Wrigley. It was a brief meeting. "He said, 'Hello, nice to meet you,'" Joan remembers. He shook their white-gloved hands, and within a week, they were under personal contract and on their way to fame and fortune.

"Double your pleasure, double your fun, with double-good, double-good, Doublemint gum," they harmonized as they promoted a product whose pleasures they were ironically denied. "I never want to see gum in the mouths of the Doublemint Twins," Philip Wrigley was heard to proclaim from his executive suite in Chicago. "My girls do not chew gum on camera."

The commercials they made extolled the joys of the great outdoors. "But we didn't know from sports!" remembers Jayne, who is the older of the two. "We were brought up with ballet and tap-dancing, and once in a while we did a cartwheel and almost killed ourselves. But they had us out on a toboggan, tossing snowballs, and trying to hit a tennis ball. They went so far as to hire Sonja Henie's partner to teach us how to ice-skate. But even after taking lessons for six weeks, we were still holding on to the barre. We were hopeless! We couldn't even learn to ride a bike. At the end, they had a bicycle built for two and had to tie it to a truck."

For girls who weren't good at sports, the Boyd sisters were good sports indeed. They survived torn cartilage, broken bones, pneumonia, and, ultimately, the termination of their contract when Joan got married and pregnant.

"And now," adds Jayne, "we get so mad at the new Doublemint commercials. What are those twins doing? Walking around a pool!"

~

Hollywood has always had a thing for two-faced women and a love of the tricky process shot. In 1946, the industry did a double take and produced two movies about twins.

"Why are you so much more beautiful than your sister?" psychiatrist Lew Ayres mused after he'd solved the puzzling case of Olivia de Havilland vs. Olivia de Havilland in *The Dark Mirror*. Within a convoluted plot involving murder and psychology, Olivia was fascinating in a subtle depiction of the outwardly identical Terry and Ruth Collins.

Maria Montez slithered into theaters as *Cobra Woman* (bad) and her identical twin sister, Tollea (good). With its far-fetched plot—involving one princess kidnapped in infancy, the other ruling an exotic South Sea island, and Lon Chaney overseeing the proceedings as a mute guard—this filmic fandango had little to do with the sisterly bonding experience and a lot to do with exposing the B-movie beauty of the sultry Ms. Montez.

The forties kept turning them out, no matter how thankless the results. "An almost totally negligible musical," grumbled James Agee of *Here Come the Waves*. Paramount's contribution to the twin oeuvre starred Betty Hutton as twin Waves, reserved Rosemary and saucy Susie. But the musical's *music* wasn't negligible. With a score by Harold Arlen and Johnny Mercer, it included the upbeat anthem, "Accentuate the Positive," and encouraged a rush of new recruits.

From the sea to the slopes, silver-screen twinship traveled off in another direction in *Two-Faced Woman*. In a casting stretch that sadly backfired, Greta Garbo danced the rumba and cavorted atypically in a performance, groused *Time* magazine, that was "almost as

Hayley Mills and Hayley Mills in The Parent Trap

shocking as seeing your mother drunk." Instead of forging new celluloid opportunities for the Swedish star, this overwrought comedy—about an introverted ski instructor trying to reactivate her husband's interest by pretending to be her own fictitious twin sister—grounded her career prematurely, when she was only thirty-six.

Playing twins was a good career move for Hayley Mills, however. In Disney's 1964 hit, *The Parent Trap*, she played identical daughters attempting to reunite their divorced parents. When they accidentally met at summer camp after being separated for years, Hayley & Hayley concocted a clever scheme revolving around mistaken identity.

Les Demoiselles de Rochefort (*The Young Girls of Rochefort*) was a French tribute to the American musical, in which real-life regular sisters Catherine Deneuve and Françoise Dorleac played on-screen twin sisters. The movie, which co-starred Gene Kelly and a score by Michel Legrand, was set on the French coast. It featured the picturesque sisters as music teachers who danced, searched for love, and did a fetching production number called "We're a Pair of Twins." Tragically, the film was released in 1968 under a shadow. Soon after shooting was completed, the young Dorleac was killed in an automobile accident.

Double exposure continued to be a draw. *Big Business*, a comedy starring Bette Midler and Lily Tomlin, did big business in 1987. Each played a pair of identical twins separated at birth by an oblivious nurse in a backwoods hospital. To make matters more confusing, Bette's two characters were both named Sadie, and Lily's both named Rose. Plenty of farcical confusion, costume changes, and state-of-the-art process shots ensued when the four met up years later at the Plaza Hotel. The mix-

Catherine Deneuve (left) and Françoise Dorleac
as The Young Girls of Rochefort

43

and-match quartet realigned in the proper biological configuration and lived happily ever after.

~

But when it came to playing sisters, the best Bette was Bette Davis. Beginning with the well-forgotten *Bad Sister* of 1931 and ending with *The Whales of August* of 1987, she became a sisterly industry in herself. In the first, based on *The Flirt* by Booth Tarkington, she played the role of woebegone Laura Madison, who stayed at home while her sister gadded about. In the last, she played the cranky sister of mild-mannered Lillian Gish.

Although *The New York Times* called her portrayal in *Bad Sister* "too lugubrious," she unhesitatingly picked up the sororal cloak again seven years later. As the eldest and sweetest of *The Sisters* in 1938, she survived marriage to Errol Flynn as well as the San Francisco earthquake. She also survived the indignity of being paid half of what Flynn made.

Firmly fixed on the sisterly path, she went on to produce and star in a remake of *A Stolen Life* for Warner Bros. In the 1939 original, Elisabeth Bergner had played identical twins Martina and Sylvina. Davis's 1946 version renamed them Kate and Pat and deposited them in a coastal New England town where they both fell for the same lighthouse inspector. Davis's dual performance was a tour de force and the movie earned $2.5 million at the box office—even if Walter Winchell did call it "short on logic but long on heart appeal" and *The Washington Daily News* "a double helping of hokum and Bette Davis."

In the days before Steadycams and computers, shooting twin scenes was no simple matter. In order to serve a double helping of Bette Davis, every dual scene had to be shot twice—with Davis and her double in one setup, followed by the double and Davis in positions reversed. The two takes were then spliced together. This procedure worked well enough to provide the illusion of one twin lighting the other twin's cigarette, of the two chatting in a garden, sailing in a boat, dancing at a party, and standing side by side as one twin watched her sister say, "I do."

Rivals and over-the-hill actresses in real life, Bette Davis and Joan Crawford teamed up in 1962 to play rivals and over-the-hill actress sisters in *What Ever Happened to Baby Jane?* The horror show was a hit, in great part because of Davis's whining vulgarity and flamboyant lack of vanity.

Thrilled by its success, Warner Bros. swiftly came up with yet another sister act for Davis in 1964. The new vehicle was a reworking of *La Otra*, a 1946 Spanish-language film starring Dolores del Rio as twins—and the plot wasn't the only thing that got reworked. The title itself probably went through more revisions than the script. According to James Spada in his 1993 Davis bio, beleaguered writers grappled with *Dead Pigeon, Scream!, Duel Me Deadly, The Fake and the Phony, Hate the Sin,* and *The Murder of Myself* before finally settling on the more upbeat *Dead Ringer.*

In this, her grand finale in the twin game, Davis played not just a twin, not just a creepy twin, but two murderous twins—one of whom killed the other, the other of whom had already killed someone else. In the dual roles of Edith and Margaret, the indefatigable Davis was beside herself.

Bette Davis
times two in
Dead Ringer

45

The Dolly Sisters, circa 1908

Three

S I S T E R   A C T

✳ ✳ ✳ ✳ ✳ ✳ ✳ ✳ ✳ ✳ ✳ ✳ ✳

At the turn of the century, entertainment was of the local variety. The circus came to town, the all-male minstrel show strutted its stuff, the burlesque sashayed in with feathers and flesh, and then vaudeville!

Fifty golden years of Weber & Fields, the Three Keatons, the Four Cohans, the six Brown Brothers, and sisters by the score! Vaudeville was a ravenous creature, trolling for talent. Bookers, scouts, and scalliwags crisscrossed the country sniffing out talent shows and beauty pageants, dance recitals and musicales.

One thing they found in profusion was the Sister Act. Down on the farm, out on the stoop, home on the range, young sisters were dressing up, prancing around, tapping and miming and harmonizing. When they showed a certain promise, they were put on stage. Talent was one thing. Having soft ringlets, beribboned braids, starched pinafores, freckled noses, and dimpled knees was a bonus—especially when attached to a set of twinkle-toed sisters who could belt out a tune.

Gender mattered more than talent. "Audiences would rather see a mediocre sister act than a good brother act," observed Joe Laurie, Jr., in his colorful chronicle, *Vaudeville.* "The women out front could either pan the girls' hair-dos or their clothes, and maybe copy them. They could argue about, 'Which is the youngest?' and 'I wonder are they real sisters?'" Usually, they *were,* but in the frantic scramble to cash in on a potentially profitable trend, the same kind of crafty mother or manager who would keep an adolescent girl in pigtails and pinafore might even go so far as to concoct a sibling relationship where previously none had existed.

The Courtney Sisters (left) and other sisters in the spotlight

With the almost simultaneous appearance of the French Twins and the Raymond Sisters on the vaudeville stage, the sister act was off and running—from A (the Aber Twins, the Alfretti Sisters, the Armstrongs, the Austins) to W (the Washbournes, the Watsons, the Wetsons, the Wilsons). The most outstanding W was the Whitman Sisters, the first famous black sister act in history, who toured the southern loop of the vaudeville circuit around 1900.

Sisters by the swarm skated and skipped rope, rode cycles and dove into tanks, swallowed fire and threw boomerangs, juggled axes and chopped wood, twirled with bears and squeezed the concertina. Nellie & Sara Kouns were twin-voiced sopranos, the Angela Sisters had a whistling act, the Emily Sisters plied the trapeze, the Hegedus Sisters fiddled, the DeVan Sisters wrapped themselves around a ladder. The Ioleen Sisters were sharpshooters who swung from a high wire, and the Transfield Sisters played glass bottles like a xylophone. And the four Allen Sisters, singing and dancing Irish jigs, had, among them, one Gracie (who would grow up to marry George Burns).

In the midst of this sororal cavalcade, several acts rose above the tambourines and fa-la-la. The spotlight shone especially bright on the Duncan Sisters. Rosetta and Vivian, the daughters of a Los Angeles real-estate agent, took to the stage in 1916 with a yodeling act; in 1922, they had a hit with "Baby Sister Blues." The next year, they found their calling in a freely adapted musical-comedy version of *Uncle Tom's Cabin.* As *Topsy and Eva*, it opened at the Alcazar Theatre in San Francisco on the night of July 9. With Vivian as the blond Little Eva and Rosetta, in blackface, as the mischievous Topsy, the show was a sensation.

"The Duncans have class. Everything they do is surefire. The customers, figuratively hanging from the rafters, went for them hook, line and sinker," *Variety* reported. When *Topsy and Eva* was filmed as a silent in

1927, its failure to click with audiences was undoubtedly based on the fact that a musical without music wasn't much to hum about.

The Duncans popped up in two more movies—*Two Flaming Youths* and *It's a Great Life*—and kept the act going onstage. A few years later, although they were hardly newcomers, they showed up (along with Imogene Coca and Van Johnson) in *New Faces of 1936*. Their youth and top billing were gone, and so was their money, but the melody lingered on, here and there on the nightclub circuit. Until the icy night of December 1, 1959, when Rosetta was in a horrific automobile accident. She died three days later, at the age of fifty-eight, and Topsy and Eva died with her.

For other kiddie acts in vaudeville, variety was the spice of life. The Roth Kids performed an array of characters. Ann was the little sister. Lillian—who would grow up to become a Ziegfeld girl, a movie star, an alcoholic, and the author of a shattering autobiography, *I'll Cry Tomorrow*, enacted on-screen by Susan Hayward—played the lead. Lillian went first, doing dramatic impersonations of famous characters. Ann followed, as a comical copycat. But offstage life was not the least bit comical.

Vaudeville "was a hard life, made up of lonely train rides," Lillian recalled, "lonely nights in strange hotels, and lonely cities in which we knew no one. 'The Roth Kids' in lights in town after town meant little to us. Wistfully, Ann and I looked out the train windows, watching the endless procession of backyard gardens flow by, catching a glimpse of little family groups, of children playing with their pets, of mother and father contentedly together on a back porch. We yearned for a home, a garden, a hammock, a sense of belonging."

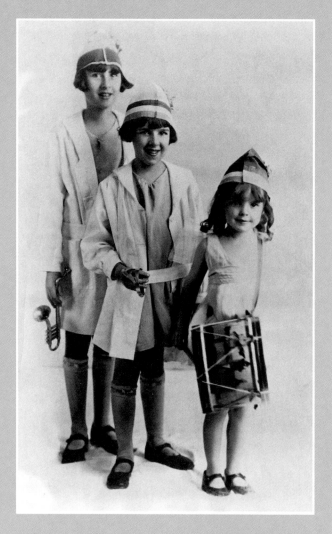

The Gumm Sisters, starring Judy Garland on drum

It was the children's hour all over America. In the twenties, the talented Gumm Sisters—Virginia, Mary Jane, and Baby Frances—took to the road in assorted kiddie revues, with a bossy mom at the helm and at the keyboard. From Grand Rapids, Minnesota, they shuffled off to Buffalo on radio's *Junior Hi-Jinx Hour* and broke into the movies just as sound entered the picture.

In 1932, when they were playing the Paramount, the balance began to change. Baby got her first *Variety* revue, and her two big sisters became a backdrop. "Gumm Sisters, harmony trio, socked with two numbers," crowed the critic. "Selling end of trio is the 10-year-old kid sister with a pip of a low-down voice. Kid stopped the show, but wouldn't give more."

Trouping from Seattle to San Diego to Denver, the sisters landed at the Oriental Theater in Chicago. There, as a last-minute replacement act, they were introduced by comedian George Jessel—not as Gumms but as Garlands. How did their new name come about? Some say it was inspired by Lily Garland, the heroine of *Twentieth Century*, playing on the same bill at the Oriental. Others believe it was a less tinseled transformation—that the sisters were named after Robert Garland, a New York drama critic who just happened to be hanging around backstage. And, since Hoagy Carmichael's "Judy" was a hit song of the moment, Baby Frances grabbed a new first name, too.

The sister act didn't last long. By 1935, it was all over for two of them. And just beginning for Judy Garland.

Koo-Kee-Koo

The Love Story of Two Birds

Introduced by the
HART SISTERS
in
Messrs Lee and
J.J. Shubert's
Musical Extravaganza
BOMBO
With Al. Jolson

Words by
King Zaney
Music by
NacioHe

WITH BEST WISHES,
The De Castro Sisters

THE SISTERS LORET

English Singing and Dancing Act

RAGTIME
(Daddy Used To Play)

RECORDED BY
THE PETERS SISTERS
ON COLUMBIA
RECORDS

CHAPPELL & CO., LTD.

2/-

POPULAR
LEO FEIST
EDITION
NEW YORK

It was another juvenile act that inspired the movie *Gypsy*—which was inspired by the Broadway musical *Gypsy*, which was inspired by the book *Gypsy*, which was written by the world's most famous stripper, Gypsy Rose Lee. *Gypsy* immortalized the kiddie sister act, the tawdry backstage life on the Orpheum Circuit, and the quintessential stage mother.

And there was none more quintessential than Mama Rose, the pushy, brazen, shamelessly ambitious mother of two dancing daughters, June and Louise. She concocted their sketches, harassed the bookers, noodged the managers, and sewed on every sequin by hand. The resulting act, "Dainty June and Company," featured the sisters Hovick and a gaggle of chorus boys dressed as newsboys, cows, and other characters.

Years past vaudeville, when June was all grown up and reinvented as actress June Havoc, she reminisced about her bespangled youth on "the happy island of vaudeville" in her own autobiography, *Early Havoc*. And in hers, Louise/Gypsy described her mother's knack at hyperbole. Using one of June's finale dresses as an example, she remembered, "On the program it was stated that the dress cost one thousand dollars, and that there were a million stones on the skirt alone. Mother wanted to add that three women went blind working on it."

To stand out from the crowd twittering and twirling on stage, an act relied on effect and invention. How else to bewitch the audience and grab the grosses? In the competitive tornado of live entertainment—with thousands of acts vying for position and billing—you had to have a gimmick.

With the Dolly Sisters, the gimmick was twinship. Promoters promoted their look-alike beauty, and bets were made from Brooklyn to Biarritz. Were they both born on October 25, 1892—or weren't they? Roszicksa (Rosie) and Jancsi (Jenny) Deutsch, petite and brunette, may or may not have been twins. Whatever the truth, there was no denying their appeal. Not only were they the most famous sister set of their day; they were among the first stars to cross the line from show business to high society.

Their publicists billed them as twins, and indeed, they seemed to be a perfect match. Born in Hungary, they grew up on New York's Lower East Side and supported themselves by teaching dance. When they made their vaudeville debut as the Dolly Sisters at New York's Keith Union Square Theater in 1909, they were spotted by the eagle-eyed Florenz Ziegfeld, who knew a double-barreled draw when he saw one. Promptly he planted them front and center in the Ziegfeld Follies of 1911, where they did a fascinating number playing Siamese twins.

Their fame was based less on their dancing toes than on their lush lifestyles, insatiable wanderlust, and the exorbitant amounts of money they made as well as the money they gambled and lost. Dukes, tycoons, castles, casinos, husbands, other people's husbands . . . the Dollys were all over the map. They broke the bank at Monte Carlo, and they broke hearts. Jenny bought jewels and won big at the races. Rosie did charity work, when she could fit it in. They starred in a 1917 silent, *The Million Dollar Dollies,* endorsed such nonessential products as Vanity Fair's jersey silk Pettibocker, and flitted around the palace with the Prince of Wales.

The decorative sisters were invited everywhere. Summoned to the White House for breakfast, they thought nothing of letting President Coolidge cool his

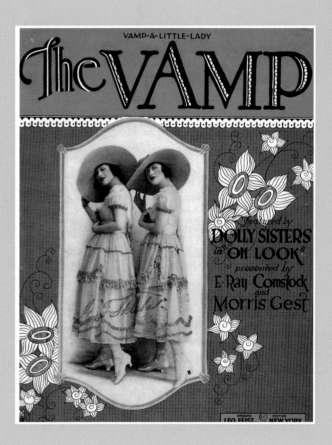

The Dolly Sisters do "The Vamp."

Theatre Magazine

TITLE REG. U. S. PAT. OFF.

35 Cents
$3.50 a Year

FEBRUARY, 1918
VOL. XXVII. NO. 204

© Photo
Sarony

DOLLY SISTERS

heels until they were sufficiently wide awake. "Who's he? A Vermont farmer," they snapped when it was time to set out. "We don't start working until we have our coffee."

Whirling through the twenties, the Dolly Sisters introduced the Charleston and the Black Bottom to ardent New York audiences at the Jardin de Paris, and zigzagged to the Moulin Rouge in Paris and to London's West End for more. When they played the Palace on Broadway, they were billed as "Twin-Souls of Gracefulness and Elusive Charm." In *The Greenwich Village Follies of 1924*, their showstopper, "The Dollies and the Collies," featured trained dogs imitating them. The twenties roared to a close, and the sister act retired from the stage.

In 1933, Jenny and a lover were en route to Paris when there was a disastrous auto accident. The details were never made clear. Jenny survived and spent the next eight years in and out of hospitals, trying to restore her shattered beauty and spirit. Alas, she could not. In 1941, at the Shelton apartments in Los Angeles, Jenny Dolly was found dead at forty-eight. With a curtain sash, or the living-room drapes, or a shower rod (according to varying reports), she had hanged herself. Rosie lived on for thirty years until she died of heart failure. Together again, the Dollys now reside in the Great Mausoleum at Forest Lawn.

As a postscript to their glory days, 20th Century-Fox came up with a splashy musical tribute. But when Betty Grable and June Haver portrayed them in 1945,

Betty Grable and June Haver as movieland's Dolly Sisters

The Dolly Sisters were no longer small and dark and Hungarian; they were big and blond and Hollywood.

~

Lillian and Dorothy Gish were small and delicate and in the right place at the right time. By the turn of the century, they were child actresses emoting with precocious flair in touring melodramas—*In Convict's Stripes, East Lynne, At Duty's Call, Editha's Burglar, The Child Wife.*

And nothing fazed them. "It doesn't hurt a bit to be flung into the cage, and I'm not afraid," five-year-old Dorothy boasted to a reporter about co-starring with two live lions in *Her First False Step*, a part she had taken over from Lillian, who was now six and a half.

Constantly moving in and out of new cities and old boardinghouses, the sisters lived with their mother, who helped support the family by taking a few bit parts herself. Along the melodrama circuit, they met up with Mary Pickford, and in 1912 she led them to D. W. Griffith and the world of silent movies.

In a brownstone on East Fourteenth Street in New York City, this lanky genius was busy making newfangled one- and two-reelers and inventing an industry for which pretty little girl actresses were very much in demand. "I remember one day in the early summer going through the gloomy old hall of the Biograph Studio," he wrote years later of their meeting, "when suddenly all gloom seemed to disappear. This change in atmosphere was

Dorothy (left) and Lillian Gish looking wistful
Opposite: The Gish girls with their mentor, D. W. Griffith,
leaving the White House after lunch with President and Mrs. Harding

caused by the presence of two young girls sitting side by side on a hall bench. They were blondish and were sitting affectionately close together. I am certain that I have never seen a prettier picture."

He hired them on the spot, and by that afternoon they were before the camera playing two sisters in *An Unseen Enemy.* Bewitched by their sisterness but unable to tell them apart, he replaced their black hair ribbons with a blue one for Lillian and a red one for Dorothy. He also attempted to change their name from "Geesh," as he teasingly pronounced it, to something more sentimental (Bessie Love and Blanche Sweet were two popular actresses of the day). The Gishes declined.

As members of the Biograph stock company, the sisters churned out picture after picture after picture. Lillian, looking wistful and woebegone, was the perfect heroine for Griffith's groundbreaking twelve-reel epic *The Birth of a Nation* and his eight-hour extravaganza *Intolerance.* While she was being beaten to death in *Broken Blossoms* and riding an ice floe in *Way Down East,* Dorothy—who had a bouncier affect—was starring in her own comedy series, playing such spunky females as *Battling Jane, Peppy Polly,* and *Flying Pat.*

In 1920, Lillian directed Dorothy in *Remodeling Her Husband;* Dorothy briefly remodeled her life by marrying a real-life husband, her leading man. In 1922, the Gish sisters reunited on-screen to play French Revolutionary sisters in *Orphans of the Storm.* During the next eight years, they acted in nearly twenty films. For them, silents were still golden.

When they turned to talkies—Lillian in *One Romantic Night,* Dorothy in *Wolves*—it was a turning point in more ways than one. Both movies, made in 1930, were flops. Their voices worked, but voices

weren't enough. Something more distracting and upbeat was needed to dilute the Depression. The time was right for Fred and Ginger, Mae West and W. C. Fields, suggestive chorus lines and double entendres. The very attributes that had made the Gishes huge stars of the silents—their dreamy faces, rosebud lips, angelic clouds of hair, and melancholy eyes—were just the opposite of boffo box office. Gishish earnestness was out of sync.

After years away from the theater, they chose to return in such classic vehicles as *Uncle Vanya, Camille, Hamlet, Morning's at Seven,* and *Life with Father,* moving smoothly back and forth from east to west, from stage to screen. In 1956, they toured together in *The Chalk Garden*—and took their last bow as a sister act.

Dorothy died in 1968, with her sister at her bedside. Lillian continued working and made *The Whales of August,* her 106th and final movie, at ninety-three. When she died at ninety-nine, her will established the generous Dorothy and Lillian Gish Prize for outstanding achievement in the performing arts. As had always been her style, she named it by putting her sister first.

The Gish sisters had been everything to the movies—and to each other. "The tradition which has grown up around Lillian seems to be that she is a shy helpless bit of fragility, drifting around in a sweet gentle daze," Dorothy once wrote about her big sister. "Anyone who has tried kicking Lillian has discovered the solidity of that resistance. Life has stubbed its toe, often and often, trying to disorganize her stability. She remains steadfast, unshaken, imperturbable."

"I envy this dear darling Dorothy with all my heart, for she is the side of me that God left out," Lillian responded. "The world to her is a big picnic with a great merry-go-round and lots of popcorn and wonderful balloons."

~

The lights of vaudeville were dimming. The movie lights were bright but silent. By the 1920s, the radio waves were crackling with sound. Music didn't have to be seen to be heard.

The sisterly blend had a special kind of sound: close harmony born and bred in close proximity. And in the early days of radio, no set vocalized with a smoother blend than the Boswell Sisters from New Orleans. While still in their teens, Martha, Helvetia, and Connee won a radio contest and made a few records. In the 1930s, they hit it big on a popular NBC show, *Music That Satisfies.* "Shout, Sister, Shout," which they recorded in 1931, became their theme song, and then came "Stardust," "Shine On, Harvest Moon," and "When I Take My Sugar to Tea." Wherever they sang, and with whatever orchestra—the Dorsey Brothers, Red Nichols, Victor Young—the Boswells were the most popular singing group on radio.

"We all loved the Boswell Sisters. The Boswells had broken the barrier between semi-classical and New Orleans jazz for white singers. We imitated them—even their accents." So remembered Maxene Andrews, who, along with her sisters, LaVerne and Patty, took over the singing-sister slot.

The Andrews Sisters lit up the late thirties and early forties, and their upbeat swing style on the radio, jukebox, and movie screen helped swing America through the war. In 1937, they stepped into the Decca recording studio and out into the spotlight. "Bei Mir Bist Du Schoen" was their surprisingly successful vehicle. Selected merely to fill the flip side of a record (a Gershwin tune was on

"How about a Coke"

The Andrews Sisters and the Coca-Cola Company make the most of their 1944 hit, "Rum and Coca-Cola."

the A side), this Yiddish song was an odd assignment indeed for three Gentile girls of Greek and Norwegian stock. They'd been touring as a trio, honing their harmony in this club and that. They'd come to New York, hung out at the Brill Building, snagged a spot at the Hotel Edison. Their first record had sold only three copies. But this one catapulted them to the top.

Their enthusiastic style was contagious, and they were soon a national treasure. "We were the first harmony group ever to move," Maxene recalled. "Harmony groups at that time would get around a microphone and put their heads together and get a beautiful blend. But we danced a lot. When we were singing, we couldn't stand still."

In their heyday, the Andrews Sisters were the number-one girl group in the country. They had thirty-three top-ten hits and sold over fifty-million records—including "Beer Barrel Polka," "Rum and Coca-Cola," "Don't Sit Under the Apple Tree," "Don't Fence Me

In," "Pistol-Packin' Mama," and "Boogie Woogie Bugle Boy." Off the record and on screen, they appeared as themselves in twenty-two movies, including *Follow the Boys, Hollywood Canteen,* and *Road to Rio.*

After LaVerne's death, Patty and Maxene appeared together on Broadway. *Over Here* ran for a year, providing entertainment backstage as well as out front. Pit men and prop men were aghast at the ugly squabbles and unsisterly shenanigans. By 1974, the singing sisters were decidedly out of tune. When *Over Here* was over, so was the sister act.

As the Andrews Sisters epitomized the 1940s with their padded shoulders and patriotic pep, the poodle-skirted fifties belonged to the McGuire Sisters. They emerged from middle America—specifically, from Middletown, Ohio, where Dad was a steelworker and Mom was pastor of the First Church of God. Discovered by a savvy agent at a Dayton revival meeting, the three sisters—Christine, Dorothy, and

Phyllis—zoomed to national fame in 1952 when they sang "Pretty-Eyed Baby" and broke the applause meter on Arthur Godfrey's *Talent Scouts*.

They became regulars on his weekly television show, along with Julius LaRosa, Frank Parker, Marion Marlowe, and hula girl Haleloke. In no time, "the Three Little Godfreys" became big. They were in their twenties, dressing identically, trying to look like the triplets they weren't. In 1958, they made the covers of *Look* and *Life*. Their hits were huge and included "Sugartime," "Something's Gotta Give," "Picnic," and "The Naughty Lady of Shady Lane." And soon the ladies were acting pretty naughty themselves.

Dorothy, who was married, dallied with LaRosa. Phyllis took up with mobster Sam Giancana. Both events distressed the many fans who idolized the McGuires as the models of all-American goodness. In the golden days of television, image was everything—and theirs was getting tarnished.

In a brief polishing attempt, they hooked up with squeaky-clean Pat Boone, appeared on *The Ed Sullivan Show*, then found their niche on the nightclub circuit. After Giancana was gunned down in 1975, Phyllis, going solo, mourned him melodically with the hit song, "I Don't Want to Walk Without You." Dorothy married an oil man and briefly wandered from the family group to take the part of Marmee in a 1979 TV version of *Little Women*. Chris got married and divorced four times. And as recently as 1996, the songbirds, still sporting matching gowns and hairdos, were piping away at the Westbury Music Fair, on the bill with comedian Alan King.

On another channel, America was becoming intoxicated by Lawrence Welk and his champagne bubbles. And the Lennon Sisters. Their meteoric rise was set in motion by an innocent date. Lawrence Welk, Jr., put in a persuasive word to Dad, and soon sixteen-year-old Dianne and her younger sisters—Peggy, Kathy, and Janet—were invited to join the Welk television family. The Lennons made their debut on Welk's Christmas Eve show in 1955 and stayed for years. By 1969, they were starring in their own series on ABC.

With their winning ways and sugar-coated smiles, the California goody-goodies were an enormous hit. "Already they're so normal that it hurts," sniped *TV Guide* in 1958. "Family fun in the girls' eyes consists of many things. Of birthdays and church socials. Of consuming 91 quarts of milk every week without half trying. And of baby showers, Eddie Fisher records, cook-outs, boys and sports."

The wholesome Lennons inspired full skirts with crinolines, hairstyles with bangs, and family values. Their father, Mr. Lennon, gave up his career as a dairy salesman to manage their affairs and choose the songs they sang. He protected them in real life and never let them out of his sight. In fact, he chaperoned them right into a Dell comic book of 1959. Driving to an engagement at the annual state fair, the Lennon Sisters helped solve "The Mystery of Lonesome Farm" and warbled all the way home, with Dad at the wheel.

Sisters in a set. When they were good, they were very very good. And when they were bad, they were horrid.

Take the Cherry Sisters . . . please. When Effie, Addie, Ella, Jessie, and Lizzie clumped across a stage, the sister act veered from the cheered to the jeered. It all began in Marion, Iowa. Hoping to raise money for a trip to the World's Fair of 1893, the farm girls produced a melodrama called *The Gypsy's Warning*. Encouraged by the neighbors, they took their amateurish act to Chicago. There, a visionary agent booked them on the midwestern circuit.

Out-of-towners were less charitable than the folks back home. Hugs and kisses were replaced by rotten reviews and, shockingly, rotten vegetables pitched by outraged members of the audience. So miffed were the Cherrys that they sued for slander. In Creston, Iowa, they sued the city. In Cedar Rapids, the local gazette.

Nonetheless, on they went, toting their trunks, removing tomato stains from their calicoes. In 1896 their intrepid talentlessness paid off. Gaining exposure and provoking amusement, the clodhopping group—sometimes they were five, sometimes four, and sometimes three—caught the interest of impresario Oscar Hammerstein, currently down on his luck.

"I've been putting on the best talent and it hasn't gone over," he is said to have said. "I'm going to try the worst." Plucking the Cherrys from their tour, he brought them to New York for $100 a week.

Something Good, Something Sad was a huge hit in a horrifying way. It opened on November 16, 1896, to an audience stunned by its shrieking incompetence. The Charming (and sometimes Celebrated) Cherry Sisters posed in tableaux and carried on valiantly. Jessie, wrapped in the American flag, sang "Corn Juice" and banged a bass drum. Effie sang "Three Cheers for the Railroad Boys." Addie recited an essay called "The Mystery of the Nineteenth Century."

Critics were incensed. "An experiment of a peculiar and unusual sort was tried in the Olympia Music Hall last night," snarled the *New York Times* man, "and the great crowd of people who watched it must have wondered, at its conclusion, whether the emotion they felt was pity for the four wretched women whose sorry antics had excited the derisive laughter of a few callous spectators, or whether it was shame at having come to see what they had been told beforehand would be merely an exhibition of folly and weakness."

The Cherry Sisters were an unlikely hit, and the canny Hammerstein was back in business. To ensure the success of his quirky treasure, the producer hired people in the audience to keep the vegetables flying. Soon theatergoers were bringing in produce of their own; aiming at the Cherrys had become the New York thing to do. Shielded by a mesh screen to protect them from further herbaceous onslaught, the girls were eventually earning a hefty $1,000 a week.

"The worst act in vaudeville history," as it came to be known, didn't go on for long. When Jessie died of typhoid fever in 1903, it came to a grinding halt. The remaining Cherrys went home and opened a bakery—featuring cherry pie. In the twenties, Effie ran twice for mayor of Cedar Rapids on an anti-tobacco, anti-liquor, anti-everything-of-the-moment platform. Not surprisingly, the voting populace turned her down, so she and Addie tried a couple of fruitless theatrical comebacks. Addie died in 1942 and Effie two years later.

"How wonderful a thing for the theater were the Cherry Sisters!" elegized the *New York World-Telegram* a week after Effie's death. "It was their business to receive abuse and ridicule. They summed up in themselves, and took the blame for, all the bad acting in the world.

"May the souls of the Cherry Sisters rest in peace!" Amen.

A turn-of-the-century trade card celebrating the curiosity of the sideshow

TWO-HEADED LARK

Four

March of the

SIAMESE TWINS

❃ ❃ ❃ ❃ ❃ ❃ ❃ ❃ ❃ ❃ ❃ ❃ ❃ ❃ ❃ ❃ ❃ ❃ ❃ ❃

Conjoined twins are born on the average of three times a century. A single egg on its way to dividing into identical twins fails to go all the way, so that the two people who develop from it remain connected by tissue and bones. Because of the rarity of those who do manage to survive, attention has historically been paid. So has the admission fee. Thanks to the wiles of greedy impresarios eager to satisfy a public appetite for the queer and quirky, the exploitation of conjoined twins has been colorful, lucrative, and cruel.

They came to be called "Siamese" simply because the first pair to become famous were born in Siam. Chang and Eng arrived on May 11, 1811. Not only were they connected by a cartilaginous band, they would eventually be connected by a wedding band— when they married a set of sisters.

As young boys, they were athletic and strong and were happy to perform all sorts of tricky feats. Such a popular curiosity did they become that they were received by King Rama III at his gilded palace in Bangkok, then sailed from Siam to Boston. Once there, Americans paid top dollar to ogle them, while Harvard doctors discussed dissecting them. But by choice, and by anatomy, the Siamese twins were inseparable.

Billing themselves as "The United Brothers," Chang and Eng created an acrobatic act and made the grand tour. In England, they were admired. In France, where it was believed that the sight of such oddity might cause undue harm to a pregnant woman and her unborn child, they were banned. Back in America, P. T. Barnum displayed them in his New York museum. When they had saved $60,000, they took charge of their own career(s) and moved on. In their late twenties, ready to settle down, they emigrated to North Carolina. They raised corn and hogs, ran a country

The Bunkers pose for Mathew Brady. Left to right: *Sarah Ann, Eng and Chang, Adelaide.* In front: *Albert and Patrick Henry, two of their twenty-two children*

store, built a big house, and, like their southern counterparts, owned slaves.

In April 1843, they also took on the name of Bunker—and took on a love life as well, becoming simultaneously infatuated with Miss Adelaide Yates, an unattached female from Wilkes County. As Mark Twain put it, in a spoof he wrote of the famous pair, "Each tried to steal clandestine interviews with her, but at the critical moment the other would always turn up." In fact, Addie preferred Eng. Hoping to placate Chang, she fixed him up with her sister, Sarah Ann. Against all odds, love won the day. In April of 1843, a double wedding took place on the grounds of their pretty North Carolina home.

The brides soon wearied of their new living arrangement. Before long, the wacky quartet was set up in two separate households a mile apart. Abiding by a schedule that never varied, they'd spend three days at Chang's place, then three at Eng's, and so on. The result was a feat to be reckoned with: two wives and twenty-two children. On January 17, 1874, at the age of sixty-two, Chang suffered a cerebral hemorrhage and died in his sleep, according to the autopsy report. Alas, poor Eng. Ready or not, he followed within hours.

⁓

Although the term "Siamese twins" originated with Chang and Eng in the nineteenth century, the actuality of conjoined twins has existed, of course, from the dawn of time. The earliest recorded pair of fastened females were England's Chulkhurst sisters, of

The first sister set in conjoined history

Biddenden, Kent. Bound at the hip, Eliza and Mary were born to wealthy parents in 1100. A medieval etching of the Biddenden Maids makes them look rather like homemade, scissor-cut paper dolls. Or, more appropriately, cookie-cutter cookies.

They expired in 1134 and left a charming legacy. Bequeathing twenty acres of profitable land to the local parish, they instructed that the rental fees benefit the poor in perpetuity. In addition, once a year, on Easter Sunday, special cakes commemorating their symmetrical generosity would be baked and distributed. The offering of these simple treats, decorated with the sisters' fetching double image, became a quaint holiday custom in one small corner of England. Nine centuries later, it still is.

Opposite in every way were the early lives of Millie and Christine, born into slavery on July 11, 1851. They, too, were joined at the buttocks, each having her own torso, arms, legs, and nervous system. They lived on a North Carolina plantation with their family until word of their odd existence leaked out. Thus began a frightful chain of events to rival the fictional *Perils of Pauline*.

Purchased from their master and whisked away from their family, they were shunted about from one town to the next, exhibited surreptitiously in darkened rooms and tattered tents. Everybody wanted to grab and snatch and cash in. An eagle-eyed promoter named Joseph P. Smith took over their management. Alas! One day, when he was away on business, Millie and Christine were stolen! For three frustrating years, Smith, the girls' despairing mother, and a detective hunted for them up and down the East Coast.

Millie and Christine, on stage and carnival poster

Following a trail from the New York docks to a dusty hall in Birmingham, the search party found the "United African Twins" singing and dancing and generally causing a sensation in the United Kingdom. They even charmed Queen Victoria at her lodge on the Isle of Wight.

When they returned to America, under the aegis of Mr. Smith, they were taught to read and write by Mrs. Smith, who also helped them hone their act. Now billed as the "Double-Tongued Nightingale," with two lovely voices joined in intricate harmony, they warbled, strummed the guitar, and bewitched audiences when they danced the schottische. They even put in a teenage appearance at Barnum's establishment in 1866.

The conjoined twins were amazingly graceful, even if their reviewers were awkward in trying to describe them. Were they an it, or was it a them? The *Liverpool Daily Courier* called Millie-Christine both "a young lady" and "two young ladies rolled into one." Perhaps they themselves were confused. As one of their ditties put it:

> I'm happy, quite, because I'm good;
> I love my Saviour and my God;
> I love all things that God has done,
> Whether I'm created two or one.

Their curious act earned them between $600 and $1,000 a week and drew audiences in astounding numbers. "One of the greatest novelties we have had with us for years, is the Two-Headed Woman at Tremont Temple," exclaimed the *Boston Sunday Gazette* in

Josefa and Rosa Blazek with Franz

1868. "She has been examined by some of our best doctors and they have pronounced it the most Wonderful Exhibition of its kind since the Siamese Twins, and even far ahead of them."

At the turn of the century, after a remarkable run, the twins bought the very plantation on which they'd been born. There they lived happily, among their fourteen brothers and sisters, until the inevitably shared final act. Millie contracted tuberculosis, and in the fall of 1912 she died. Seventeen hours later, Christine joined her. On their shared gravestone these poignant words were carved:

A SOUL WITH TWO THOUGHTS.
TWO HEARTS THAT BEAT AS ONE.

~

From womb to tomb, the problems of conjoined twins go beyond the physical. Where does one person end and two begin? Where does the "self" reside? Do conjoined twins pay one fare or two? Do they apply for one Equity card or two? One marriage license or two? Or none at all?

For Rosa and Josefa Blazek, alas, it was none at all. Being joined at the spine and pelvis may have stopped this Czechoslovakian twosome from marrying, but it didn't stop them from wiggling, waggling, climbing trees, and otherwise rising above the difficulties inherent in their plight. They were born in 1878, and in those days the most profitable career opportunities for such "special people" were the side show, the circus, the circuit. So the Blazek twins learned several languages,

played the violin, cello, piano, and xylophone, and eventually wound up on the vaudeville stages of Paris, London, New York, and Mitteleuropa.

The Blazeks longed for normal love, and one of them found it . . . for a while. Rosa got pregnant in Prague (although Josefa continued to menstruate). Rosa's lover offered to marry her, or her sister, or both. But church and state officials decreed that a wedding was out of the question; one man could not enter into holy matrimony with what added up to two women.

The pregnancy was, inevitably, a combined endeavor. Rosa delivered a normal, healthy, nine-pound boy, and he became community property. The new mother may not have had a husband, but she did have live-in help. Not only was her sister there—always, always there—to help out with cradle-rocking and lullaby-singing, she also was there to take over at mealtime. For astonishingly, she, too, was capable of nursing the baby with her own breast milk.

When the Blazeks hit the vaudeville circuit again, the act had new billing: Josefa & Rosa and Baby.

In 1922, the trio was performing in Chicago when Josefa was hit by influenza. Her life—and, two agonizing days later, Rosa's—came to an end. They were forty-four. What became of their twelve-year-old son, Franz, remains a mystery.

~

Every student of American history knows that Massachusetts produced the Lowells, the Cabots, and the Kennedys. More careful scrutiny reveals that Massachusetts also produced the Gibbs. Mary and

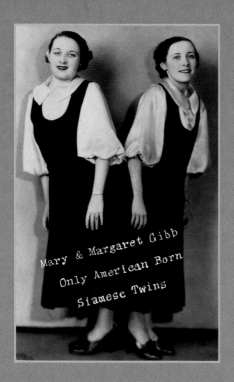

Above: *The Gibb girls and the Massachusetts hospital where they were born and died.*
Opposite: *Christmas in Manhattan, 1927. The Gibbs share Siamese-twin dolls.*

Margaret Gibb, who arrived on May 20, 1912, claimed to be the first American-born conjoined twins, although they followed Millie and Christine. As such, they led anything but a proper New England girlhood.

Seized at thirteen by a savvy seaside promoter, the girls—who were attached at the base of the spine, but were otherwise fully formed and not unattractive—made a brief foray into show business, singing and dancing on the Coney Island Bowery. When the Society for the Prevention of Cruelty to Children objected to their under-aged and over-exploited visibility, they were so mortified by the brouhaha that they returned to the sanctity of their Yankee hearth.

By sixteen, they were ready to reenter show business, as it were. They played the Loew's and Keith vaudeville circuits; they trouped across Europe. Returning to the States, they appeared at the 1933 Century of Progress Exposition in Chicago and then, not surprisingly, joined the circus—bouncing back and forth for seven years from Ringling Brothers to Cole Brothers to Ringling to Cole.

When they gave up showbiz shortly before their thirtieth birthday, what then? Their options limited, the Gibb girls returned to Holyoke. Unlike others in their peculiarly limited situation, this sister set was lucky. Not only had their supportive and protective parents accompanied them hither and yon on their theatrical rounds, but they rearranged the family house to make their daughters' longtime dream come true. The Mary-Margaret Gift Shoppe, set up in the front parlor, offered greeting cards and gewgaws, pottery and doodads. For eight years, no local baby shower was complete without rompers hand-stitched by the sisters

themselves. After closing up shop in 1950, they settled into a quiet life with their widowed mother. They died of cancer in 1967 at the age of fifty-four, two minutes apart.

～

"So much wonderment has centered around us, especially how two human beings can endure constant continuous living together harmoniously. Yet, we two, without parents, without one intimate friend until we were 24 years old, have found a fascinating and interesting life." So wrote Daisy and Violet Hilton in their compelling dual autobiography, *Intimate Lives and Loves of the Hilton Sisters*, published in 1951.

If united twins can ever be considered sexy or beautiful, then the sexiest and most beautiful were surely these two. Because they grew up in a cosmopolitan setting—nightclubs, movies, radio, books—their visibility as entertainers went beyond the limited world of the carnival and music hall.

They were born on February 5, 1908. According to varying reports, their birth occurred either in the seaside resort town of Brighton, England—or in a dusty Texas outpost. Their mother, Kate, was either an unmarried English barmaid who died or didn't die when they were born—or she was the wife of a Texas army captain. In any case, they were delivered by a woman named Mary Hilton, bar owner and midwife. It was into her manipulative grip that the terrified mother handed her strange offspring, and then fled. No fool Miss Mary, who accepted this four-armed, four-legged bundle of joy with a crafty plan up her sleeve.

Henceforth, the twins were her virtual prisoners, hidden away to ensure their value. They weren't to be seen without the privilege of being paid for. "We were very knowing and we developed opinions although we were treated like animals, living in a cage. We were kept in one room, regularly whipped, scolded and trained. We were never permitted to play with other children," they complained. Instead, they were on the road at the age of three, strutting their stuff before gawking circus audiences and obeying Auntie as well as her five husbands, all of whom they were required to call "Sir."

Home life was dissonant, but on stage there was harmony—with Daisy singing soprano and Violet alto. They expanded their repertoire, and learned to dance the Black Bottom from a young vaudevillian named Bob Hope. While still in their teens, they were touring Europe and Australia and forging backstage friendships with such headliners as Sophie Tucker, Harry Houdini, and the Duncan Sisters.

Somewhere in the mid-twenties, after bringing her protégés to America, the shrewd and cunning Auntie died. In her will she bequeathed the hapless Hilton twins to her daughter, Edith, and Edith's husband, Myer Myers—whom they were also required to call "Sir." If Auntie was controlling, these two were even more so. "Willed as an old ring or chair! It couldn't be!" they recalled in their book. "We had to work as hard, and the only privacy we were to have was in our minds. Our new owners slept in the same room with us. We were never out of their sight."

Myers had big plans. He devised a publicity pamphlet, heralding Violet and Daisy as San Antonio's Siamese Twins. "These Lovely Girls Happy and

SAN ANTONIO SIAMESE TWINS.

Above: *The Hilton Sisters toot and primp, as teenage musicians and (opposite) as grown-up glamour girls on the boardwalk in Atlantic City, 1933.*

Vivacious in Their Inseparably Linked Lives Have Perfected Natural Talents Which Make Them One of the Greatest and Most Meritorious Attractions in the World," it shouted.

The girls added the sax and ukelele to their bag of tricks and made their American vaudeville debut in February 1925. "We were big-time: 46 weeks on the Marcus Loew circuit at $2,500 a week," they wrote. And getting bigger. In 1926, they joined the Orpheum Circuit and were earning $3,850 a week. They were rich, famous, over twenty-one, living in a luxurious house in San Antonio—yet they were essentially living in slavery.

But the situation was soon to change. In a stupefying fit of jealousy, the wife of their publicist named the Hiltons as co-respondents in a divorce action— and demanded a quarter of a million dollars—all because they had written "love" on an autographed photo to him. Baffled and humiliated, they found themselves testifying in court and defending their virtue.

But this particular cloud had a silver lining. Their lawyer, the compassionate Martin J. Arnold, easily got the divorce action dismissed. Then, so moved was he by the disturbing nature of their everyday lives in captivity that he led them to an even greater victory. In a case that made headlines across the country in 1931— and would certainly have made Court TV today—the Hiltons sued their two guardians for their freedom.

Armed with a $100,000 settlement (a mere fraction of what they had earned for their captors over the years) and finally untethered, the twins set out to see the world and seek their own fortune.

Will She Pay The Ultimate Price For Her Sister's Crime?

Chained For Life

Intimate Loves and Lives of the
HILTON SISTERS
WORLD FAMOUS
SIAMESE TWINS

"For the first time we could order something on a menu which we wanted," they triumphantly wrote. "We could dress and act our age, and no longer be made up as children with bows in our hair. We got permanents and pinned up our hair. I, Violet, had always wanted to drink a cocktail. I, Daisy, wanted to smoke a cigarette. We did." They also took a luxurious apartment overlooking Central Park, slumbered in a canopy bed, shopped Fifth Avenue, and spent many a night painting the town red.

Footloose and fancy free, in a manner of speaking, the girls hit the nightclub circuit as the Hilton Sisters Revue and then went Hollywood. In 1932, they appeared in Tod Browning's *Freaks*, a cult classic that was made and then disowned by MGM. Violet and Daisy were two of the strange players in this black-and-white conglomeration of "special people."

Their film career peaked in 1951 with their second and final screen appearance in which they starred as Vivian, a brunette, and Dorothy, a blonde. Widely regarded as one of the worst movies ever made, *Chained for Life* was notable not for its ethically provocative plot (one twin is guilty of murder; how can both be sent to jail?) nor for its clunky supporting cast (a histrionic array of sharpshooters and shysters) but because it presented the Hiltons in a fictionalization of their real-life attachment. They sang in close harmony in true fifties girl-group fashion, with flouncy costumes and perky gestures—not side by side, but at the requisite 45-degree angle. But more poignant by far was an Agnes de Mille-ish fantasy sequence (accomplished with doubles) in which "Dorothy" dreamed of becoming unfastened from "Vivian" and dancing off into the sunset.

They also dreamed of romance. They were pretty, their odd togetherness was tantalizing, and they provoked a barrage of carnal curiosity. Before long, they were making up for lost time in the sex department. Asked reporters, "How do Siamese twins make love?" Replied the no-longer-shrinking Violet, "Sometimes I quit paying attention. Sometimes I read and sometimes I just take a nap. We've learned not to know what the other is doing unless it's our business to know it."

Tuning out and turning away had become a necessity. All it took was focus, an art they had learned years before from their old backstage confrère, escape artist Harry Houdini. "You must learn to forget your physical link," he had advised them. "Put it out of your mind. Work at developing mental independence of each other. Through concentration you can get anything you want."

What they wanted was to be loved. Men galore were lured by their curious charm. Some were serious, some were not. Violet and a bandleader beau tried to get a marriage license in twenty-one states. In a situation reminiscent of the Blazeks', the lovers were turned down because the bride-to-be was considered two women, not one. "The very idea of such a marriage is quite immoral and indecent," huffed the Manhattan corporation counsel, with which the bandleader gave up and bit the dust. Thanks, however, to a publicity-seeking manager who finagled a marriage license in Dallas, Violet did eventually make it to the altar—although not exactly for love. In 1936, she and her dancing partner, James Walker Moore, enthralled a crowd of 100,000 at the Texas Centennial as they took their vows on the 50-yard line of the Cotton Bowl.

As for Daisy, the maid of honor (and inescapable chaperone on the honeymoon): "They'll hardly know I'm around." The new husband wasn't around for long either, and Violet's marriage was soon annulled. When it was Daisy's turn at the altar five years later, she chose one Harold Estep, a fleet-footed component of their nightclub act. That union was even briefer. After a taste of marriage times three, Estep stepped out.

Show business was no business for middle-aged performers such as the Hiltons. As their options closed down, and their fortune dwindled, the valiant sisters sought other venues, settling for a while in Miami. Their ringlets and ruffles long outgrown, the former headliners were soon selling hamburgers and fries at the Hilton Sisters Snack Bar.

Their final engagement was even bleaker. Arriving in Charlotte, North Carolina, in 1962 to promote a showing of *Freaks* at the local drive-in, they found themselves stranded and virtually penniless. Ever resourceful, they made the best of it. They settled in at a trailer park, attended services at the Purcell Methodist Church, and found work weighing and bagging vegetables at the Park-N-Shop. United at the grocery scale they remained until 1969, when they succumbed at sixty-one to the Hong Kong flu.

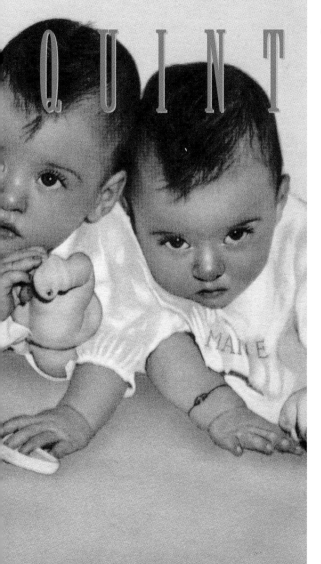

Five

A Quintessence of QUINTUPLETS

Their "mother" was a succession of nurses in white uniform. Their "father" was a brisk country doctor. Their "governesses" were the welfare minister of Ontario, the district supervisor of the Red Cross, and a court-appointed board of guardians. Their "playground" was a side-show/laboratory. Their "home" was a hospital.

They were the Dionne Quintuplets: Yvonne Edouilda Marie, Annette Lilianne Marie, Cécile Marie Emilda, Emilie Marie Jeanne, and Marie Reine Alma. Their story can be seen from many angles, but one thing is clear: They were removed from their home, made a $500-million industry by the Canadian government that would rival Niagara Falls as a tourist attraction, and were destroyed in the process.

The mid-thirties was a troubled time, beset by depression and threatened by war. The scenario was bleak, but little girls were doing their best to divert the penny-pinched public. Shirley Temple tapped away the blues in *Stand Up and Cheer*. Little Lulu and Little

Gateway to Callander, the Home of the Quintuplets, Ontario, Canada.—16.

House where the Quintuplets were born, Callander, Canada.—1.

All roads lead to Quintland.

Orphan Annie, in their cheery red dresses, skipped rope and played cartoon pranks. Little Gloria played the pawn in a public tug-of-war between mother and aunt. And on May 28, 1934, the world turned its gaze to the sensational litter of little girls just delivered on a scrubby homestead in Northern Ontario. The quinfants were an even more dazzling distraction.

They came from peasant stock. Their parents, Elzire and Oliva Dionne, were a hardworking French Catholic farm couple, simple and unsophisticated. Before the miracle birth, they had been struggling along with five young children in a ramshackle farmhouse with no electricity, running water, indoor plumbing, or telephone. They grew and sold vegetables, raised livestock, sewed their own clothes, and lived an isolated life centered around family and church. Such was the life of the devout Dionnes in the town of Corbeil, near Callander and North Bay.

Oliva Dionne owned a car; he was one of the few farmers in the area who did. And a lucky thing it was. Just before dawn, two months earlier than expected, twenty-five-year-old Elzire went into labor. She was in extreme distress. Soon there were two midwives at her bedside. Growing alarmed at her frightening condition, they sent Oliva off to fetch the doctor without delay.

But even before the doctor arrived, the first baby did. So did the second. Just as the third was beginning to emerge, Dr. Allan Roy Dafoe stepped through the front door—and into history. By the dim light of a flickering kerosene lamp, he delivered two more, although with little hope that any of them would last until sunrise. The birth of five identical babies, all developing from one egg, was more than a rare occurrence; it was only the third such birth in three centuries of recorded history.

Dazed and barely conscious, Elzire was given last rites by the local priest. Meanwhile, her babies struggled for breath. Swaddled in soft pieces of an old blanket, they nestled together in a butcher's basket, warmed by heated bricks in front of the open stove. One of the nurses described them in her journal as "premature, scrawny, rickety, hungry mites" who "sound like mosquitoes when crying." Every so often, they were massaged with warm olive oil and fed a few drops of sweetened water from an eyedropper. And whenever one of them wilted, she was given a few drops of rum.

Word was out, and within hours, the overpopulated, overheated house was under siege. Such an event could hardly be kept a secret. Busybody neighbors, newspaper reporters, and newsreel photographers were soon swarming about the Dionne place, bringing incubators, safety pins, bottles, and diapers by the dozen. Presents arrived, too, inevitably in sets of five. Because Elzire was unable to feed her new brood, mothers from Toronto, Montreal, and Chicago donated their breast milk. Everything was going on at once, swirling and twirling around the incubated quintet. And amid the hysteria—giving orders, directing traffic, granting interviews, and acting as the ringleader of this five-ring circus—was none other than the country doctor. "I'm running the show," he was fond of saying.

Dr. Allan Roy Dafoe was an unlikely candidate for stardom, a man with no apparent ambition beyond a simple rural practice. He had left Toronto, where he had been educated, to take refuge in this backwoods

Dafoe Hospital for the Dionne Quintuplets, Callander, Canada.

Dafoe Hospital and Play House of Dionne Quintuplets, Callander, Ontario, Canada.—15.

Quintland, Home of the Dionne Quintuplets.—17.

THE
Country Doctor
TALKS TO WOMEN

DR. ALLAN ROY DAFOE

The good doctor cashes in on his celebrity.

outpost. Although he'd been serving the French-speaking district for twenty-five years, he maintained his isolation by refusing to learn a word of French. This self-imposed exile was undoubtedly a result of profound insecurity. He was small, wore gloves purchased in the children's department, and had an oversized head. Even worse, he stammered badly. Living among French Catholic country folk with whom he had nothing in common, he could feel superior.

Certainly, he felt superior to Oliva Dionne. Pacing the porch, slamming doors, and tearing at his hair, Dionne was wild with worry. Within two hours, he had gone from being the father of five to the father of ten. How on earth would he ever be able to support his alarmingly enlarged family? So many babies were not a blessing but an embarrassment.

Then came an offer too good to refuse. Three mustachioed promoters, looking to cash in at the Chicago Century of Progress, sped to the farmhouse with an enticing contract in hand: $250 a week—with a first check of $100 on the spot. Would Mr. Dionne give the nod to a real-live quintuplet exhibit? It would make a fortune.

Take what you can while you can, Dr. Dafoe advised him. So the panicked father signed. Bad mistake. When the news became public, an outcry arose. How could a father agree to exhibit his own children—especially children who were only seventy-two hours old? Humiliated, he promptly returned the check. But it was too late. The deed was done, the die was cast. This sleazy contract would become the cornerstone of a civil war over the custody of the quintuplets that would rage on for nine long years.

Ignoring his previous advice and betraying Oliva Dionne, the nimble Dr. Dafoe changed his tune. "As long as I'm boss there will be no trip for these babies," he proclaimed. With no warning, Dionne's position as head of the family had been usurped, his reputation as a responsible father damaged beyond repair.

The power struggle was on. The Chicago debacle was history, but now came a new concern. How were these five fragile creatures to survive among such callous and careless people? Their welfare was all that mattered. In this corner: Dafoe, the Red Cross, the press, the public, and the English-speaking Protestant government of Ontario—all of whom felt that the babies' survival depended on separation from the family. In the other corner: Ezire and Oliva Dionne, trapped in an emotional, religious, political, and economic conundrum.

Squeezed and stigmatized, the parents had no choice. They surrendered custody of their five babies to the Red Cross and a board of guardians with the promise that *les jumelles* would be returned to their care in two years. (Wrong. In an about-face eight months later, the government would break its promise. Under "An Act for the Protection of the Dionne Quintuplets," the children would become government property and eventually wards of King George V of England.)

Immediately, a new "home" within a fenced-in compound went up one hundred yards away. As the world watched, the fragile four-month-old infants were taken from the family to their new quarters. The modern facility contained nine rooms on one floor and was named, not surprisingly, the Dafoe Hospital and

Nursery. There was also a house for the nurses, a guard-house, and an enormous parking lot. For ready or not, here came the crowds. To Quintland! "By car, by bus, by train . . . All roads lead to Callander since the arrival of the Quints!" read an ad of the moment.

Their appeal was so irresistible, their sameness so compelling, that everybody came—those who could barely afford to go anywhere and those who could well afford to go everywhere. Seeing the quints was the thing to do, and every bumper sticker proved it. To accommodate the influx of outsiders, a special walkway surrounded the children's playground. It was fitted with windows made of the newly invented one-way vision glass—for the sole purpose of gawking.

The miracle babies had survived the odds and were flourishing under Dr. Dafoe's no-nonsense guidelines—sunshine, fresh air, minimal handling, cod-liver oil, and "oxygen cocktails." Delighted with their improvement and caught up in the whirlwind of tourists and money, the doctor had conveniently forgotten his disdain for Papa Dionne's interest in exhibiting the babies at the World's Fair. Now, ironically, the fickle Dafoe was exhibiting the quints two and sometimes four times a day.

At first, the baby girls were held up by their nurses and identified by signs bearing their names. Then they were toddling, swinging, wading, building snowmen, smashing sandcastles, and otherwise performing for the public they were not supposed to know was there. "In theory, the onlookers were invisible to anyone in the playground," they recalled in their 1965 memoir, *We Were Five.* "But of course we knew very well that we were watched every minute that we spent at play there."

The Dionne Quintuplets had become North America's number-one roadside attraction and a bonanza for everybody involved. Admission was free, and so was parking, but there were still big bucks to be made. Along the road to Quintland, the hordes of daily visitors could fill up their Packards and DeSotos at Uncle Leon Dionne's gasoline station, whose five pumps were named after the babies. They could take the train and arrive at the spiffy new railroad station. They could check in at the Callander Hotel, which had added another floor, or the brand-new Red Line Inn, or any one of the two hundred tourist camps that had sprung up along the way.

Before standing in line to see the quints themselves, they could stand in line to meet the midwives at the Midwives' Souvenir Pavilion and ogle the basket that had been the babies' first bed. At Oliva Dionne's Woollen Shop, they could choose a scarf, and at Oliva Dionne's Souvenir Shop they could pay 25 cents for his autograph. They could buy a photo taken by the official Dionne photographer—and only by the official Dionne photographer, who had an exclusive contract. No one else, not even the quints' own father, could take their picture.

There was one souvenir they didn't have to buy. Pebbles, discovered lying about near the exit from the playground, had become valuable as "tokens of fertility." Before long, tons of these talismans were being pocketed by the public (and replenished daily, trucked in from nearby).

At the same time, quint life was under another kind of scrutiny. Fingerprints and footprints, hair whorls and ear shapes, gestures and grimaces, tears and

"OF COURSE—
WE EAT KARO"
the Dionne Quintuplets

POURING SPOUT

ACCEPTED
AMERICAN
MEDICAL
ASSN.
Council
on Food

copyrighted 1937, Nea Service, Inc.

*Movieland meets Quintland.
A scene from* Reunion,
the Dionnes' second film outing

tantrums, intake and output: Every mood, mannerism, and microbe was being documented and analyzed by a steady stream of professional experts. Within their controlled environment, Yvonne, Annette, Cécile, Emilie, and Marie were widely viewed as look-alike marionettes dancing merrily in tandem from dawn to dusk.

Dafoe had two right-hand advisers. Under the direction of pediatrician Alan Brown, who headed the Hospital for Sick Children in Toronto (and invented Pablum), the girls grew strong on a low-fat, high-visibility diet with a maximum of vegetables and a minimum of sweets. The man in charge of their psychological development was Dr. William E. Blatz. As director of the Institute of Child Study at the University of Toronto, his methods of child-rearing were on the cutting edge. He set up the quints' minute-by-minute schedule and nursery-school curriculum. As for punishment, whenever a quint acted up or became too boister-

ous, she was isolated from the group in a small room designated for solitary confinement.

"To Blatz, the quintuplets, landing virtually on his doorstep, must have seemed sent from Heaven especially for his benefit," wrote Pierre Berton in his fascinating account of *The Dionne Years.* "No social scientist had ever been faced with such a unique and intriguing challenge." And he made the most of it by establishing a stunningly fine-tuned series of behavioral studies and churning out two books based on his Quintland experience. Although he studied their behavior to a fare-thee-well, Blatz professed the opposite, writing that "the quintuplets could of course not be treated as guinea pigs."

Every psychologist wanted to share his expertise and add his own animal analogy. "Five little guppies living in a fish bowl may not be distracted by constant exposure. But babies are not fishes," declared the insightful Dr. Alfred Adler from Vienna. "Treating the quintuplets alike in every respect induces a uniformity which is not conducive to the development of the individual," he warned in *Cosmopolitan*. "It would be wise to dress the five children in different colors, give them different toys and even different food. They should find playmates outside; they should have frequent contacts with their brothers and elder sisters, and as little fuss as possible should be made about the fact that they are quintuplets." Nobody listened. Adler's advice might have been psychologically sound, but it was certainly not popular.

Their togetherness was not negotiable. And there were far too few contacts with the brothers and sisters. Although Dr. Dafoe had no qualms about exposing his charges to the visiting crowds, dignitaries, guardians, and celebrities, he claimed that the quints' siblings were dangerous, germ-ridden intruders. As for parental visits, they continued to be by appointment only.

No one could make a move without the doctor's say-so. Except the doctor. Responding to public demand, Dafoe packed his bag and journeyed south to cosmopolis. Grand Central Station! The Empire State Building! The Staten Island Ferry! The subway! The nightclubs! New York was his oyster, and the press his pearl. A "droll, elfin little man," Dorothy Kilgallen crowed in the *Journal*. "He thrilled the devil out of me. I mean it," rhapsodized Walter Winchell after Dafoe addressed a standing-room-only crowd at Carnegie Hall on the topic of his five little wonders and how they grew.

The deified Dafoe continued on to the nation's capital and managed to fit in a ten-minute chat at the White House with FDR. When he finally flew back to Callander, he left an adoring fan club in his wake. One

fawning reporter extravagantly suggested that "anyone's vocabulary is lacking in enough adjectives to do him justice—modest, wise, genial, friendly, cheerful, charitable, courteous, kindly, reputable, ethical—they all apply."

He was the darling of the day.

Meanwhile, the other five darlings of the day were going about their business—which was turning into big business indeed. Devotees who couldn't make the trip to Callander could certainly find the quints on Main Street, U.S.A. Barely a week went by that they didn't show up at the corner newsstand as cover girls on *Life, Liberty, Time,* or *Modern Screen*. Children could fall asleep to the gentle strains of the "Quintuplets' Lullaby." And down the block at the Bijou, no newsreel was complete without a quint update. There they were in their five-part splendor: losing a tooth, launching a ship, meeting Amelia Earhart, curtsying to the King and Queen.

The Dionnes were too hot not to handle. Manufacturers and marketers solicited their endorsement for an astounding assortment of merchandise, including Bee Hive Golden Syrup, Karo Syrup, Palmolive Soap, Quaker Oats, Lysol Disinfectant, Colgate Dental Cream, Musterole Chest Rub, Tiny Town Togs, Baby Ruth, Remington Rand Typewriters, McCormick's Biscuit, and Bodies by Fisher. Their likenesses were reproduced as dolls and paper dolls, on playing cards and postcards. And every year for many years, they graced a calendar put out by the preeminent Brown & Bigelow printing company.

Twentieth Century–Fox came bearing movie contracts. First up was *The Country Doctor* in 1936 with Jean Hersholt as the Dafoe-like "Dr. John Luke." (The role had been intended for Will Rogers before his untimely

"We started through life on a healthy foundation" THE QUINTUPLETS

Karo is the only syrup served to the Dionne quintuplets. Its maltose and dextrose are ideal carbohydrates for growing children— Allan Roy Dafoe, M.D.

World Copyright, 1938 NEA Service, Inc.

Remember:
Karo is rich in *Dextrose* the food energy sugar

First and Only CANDY Served the "Quints"!

"Oh---h...Chocolat Couvert!" —CECILE

"With Peanuts...Delicieux!" —MARIE

"And Crème Centre!" —YVONNE

"Nice and Chewy!" —ANNETTE

"Magnifique!" —EMILIE

UM-M-M! You'll agree with the "Quints" and millions of candy-wise Americans that Baby Ruth is candy at its finest! You'll love the luscious, velvety-smooth coating, the chewy caramel and tasty opera cream center, the abundance of golden, freshly roasted peanuts which make up this great candy bar. Baby Ruth is *good food*—good for you. Its ingredients are all pure, wholesome foods — nourishing and delicious. Enjoy a big bar of Baby Ruth *today!*

CURTISS CANDY COMPANY, CHICAGO, ILL.

CURTISS Baby Ruth

RICH IN DEXTROSE *Food-Energy Sugar*

"Baby Ruth, being rich in Dextrose, vital food-energy sugar, and other palatable ingredients, makes a pleasant, wholesome candy for children."

Allan Roy Dafoe, M.D.

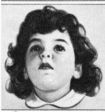

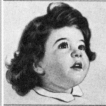

death.) The quints, who faced the cameras with great aplomb, were paid an unheard-of $50,000 (or $90 per minute), which made them the highest-paid movie stars yet. The crowd-pleaser opened big at Radio City Music Hall and was a four-star hit. But the two sequels that swiftly followed—*Reunion* and *Five of a Kind*—struck critics as a bit of a stretch. The story lines were thin, and the good-natured quints were, alas, not Shirley Temple.

They were sold as a unit, but the Dionnes were not exactly five of a kind. Within their identicality—and in spite of their handlers' rigid regimen—five separate little girls were trying to grow up. Birth order, it seemed, had already predetermined their relationship. The first born was Yvonne. As the "older sister," she seemed the most mature and self-assured. Annette, the second, was spunky and animated; she liked nature and had a bit of a temper. Cécile, born third—the middle child—was the most self-contained and independent; she could tune out her siblings and be perfectly content to play alone. Emilie, fourth, was the left-handed member of the set; mischievous clowning concealed her more serious nature. Little Marie, the last born, was, from the start, smaller and frailer than her sisters; as the "baby sister," she was accommodating and affectionate. When they played house or beauty parlor or dress-up, they tended to pair off—the two oldest and the two youngest together—with self-assured Cécile happy on her own.

∽

It was still a family divided, with the quints as center-piece. While the country doctor was riding their match-ing coattails and dispensing pediatric advice three mornings a week on CBS radio, the parents were still very much on the sidelines.

And then the tide began to turn. The initial frenzy was long over. But something was wrong. Why were five growing girls still being caged within a barbed-wire fence? And why did healthy children need nurses any-way? As for Dr. Dafoe, his image as benevolent despot of this five-star dominion was beginning to tarnish. The public was learning about all the secret commis-sions and royalties he had been slyly raking in. Above all, why was a Protestant physician, who spoke only English, continuing to control the lives of the French-speaking French-Catholic Dionne Quintuplets?

For the parents, armed with lawyers, petitions, and, at last, a swell of popular support, victory was in sight. Persistence and patience had paid off. In 1942, Dr. Dafoe visited the quints for the last time. Dethroned and failing in health, he died months later of pneumonia. In the autumn of 1943, the girls finally returned to the parental fold—nine years after they'd been taken from it. But it was far from the long-awaited happy reunion heralded by the press.

With quintuplet earnings, which had been accru-ing in a special trust fund set up soon after they were born, Oliva Dionne built a formal Georgian mansion behind a fence. The "Big House" had nineteen rooms, eight bedrooms with mirrors built into the walls, seven bathrooms, a red-carpeted library, crystal chandeliers, marble fireplaces, and furniture brought in by a Parisian decorator.

But it was too much too late. The quints dreaded rejoining a family they did not know. "The last thing

A romanticized painting from one of the wildly popular calendars published annually by Brown & Bigelow

we wanted to have to do was leave the nursery. It was a haven to us, not a prison," they recalled of their painful move. The little princesses were now Cinderellas. In a misguided attempt to bring the girls into line with the arduous family ethic, the parents Dionne soon had them scrubbing the toilets, polishing the bureaus, cleaning the floors, washing the windows, peeling potatoes, milking cows, and pitching hay.

Yvonne, Annette, Cécile, Emilie, and Marie had to learn a new kind of intimacy. Sequestered, cloistered, and virtually quarantined for nine years, they had never been allowed to play with other children; now they had to blend in with six, then seven, then eight brothers and sisters who resented them deeply. They had always slept together in one room; now they were separated, divided into pairs, with little Marie having to move in with big sister Pauline. They had been dressed and cuddled and tucked in by a government-approved team of nurses;

now they had to obey one angry, confused mother, who had no idea how to deal with these strangers who were her children.

Above all, they had to contend with their father, a man in serious conflict. Oliva Dionne had been obsessed for so long with retrieving his daughters that he had given little thought to the reality of their return. Poisoned by their defection to Dafoe and soured by the struggle, he sought to avenge his bitter frustration. With damaging inconsistency, he treated the quints as if they had betrayed him—and yet was delighted to show them off to visitors, even as they slept. What's worse, he fondled them in shockingly inappropriate ways.

The very fiveness that had made them feel special now made them feel guilty. And frightened. Their parents and siblings were physically and mentally abusive, as if blaming them for their multiple birth and the

93

expense of their upkeep. "It was," the quints remembered, "the saddest home we ever knew."

They attended high school across the road at the Villa Notre-Dame (formerly the Dafoe Hospital and Nursery); their few classmates had been handpicked by the nuns. And at eighteen, after graduating from high school, they finally cleared the fence. Breaking away from their parents' malevolent grip, they went off on their own for the first time in their lives—to a Catholic college in the town of Nicolet.

Then came the nearly impossible task of separating from one another. On their nineteenth birthday, Marie announced her decision to enter a convent. Soon thereafter, Emilie, too, chose to take holy orders. But serenity was not to be. Shockingly, tragically, within months of her arrival, she was dead at the age of twenty. And a deep, dark family secret was revealed. Emilie had been an epileptic since puberty. All alone in her cloistered room, she had suffered a seizure. Without her sisters there to save her, she had suffocated.

The famous five were now four, irreparably diminished. Nonetheless, they moved ahead toward independence. In Montreal, they studied music, art, nursing. Several times, Yvonne tried unsuccessfully to become a nun. Marie left her convent to study literature, then suffered a nervous breakdown. Although she managed to open a flower shop, which she named Salon Emilie, she was not able to make it flourish.

Success in marriage also eluded the Dionnes. Cécile and Annette both wed the first men they ever dated, and both were eventually divorced. When Marie's marriage also ended, she slid into an irreversible depression and died of a stroke at thirty-five. (Despite an early prediction by a biologist who had arrogantly declared that the quintuplets would never be able to give birth, they were successful at having children and produced ten among them.)

The "Big House" became a nursing home. The farmhouse was moved to North Bay and opened as a museum. As for the surviving quints, Yvonne, Annette, and Cécile live modestly these days in the Montreal suburb of St. Bruno. Free at last—Oliva Dionne died in 1979 and Elzire in 1986—they continue to be haunted by financial and emotional woes.

Emboldened by time and the death of their parents, they are attempting to exorcise their demons. *Family Secrets*, published in 1995, is the story they were afraid to tell and only alluded to in their 1965 memoir. They claim that Mom slapped them around, read their diaries, played favorites, even forbade them to sing . . . that Dad and at least one of their older brothers abused them sexually time and again. Determined to overcome their victimization, they have also filed a $10-million lawsuit against the Ontario government for an equitable share of the money they earned as babies on parade. By taking action to right the wrongs that were done them, perhaps they will finally find inner peace.

The Dionnes ride off into an idealized future.

Birthday Greetings

Sing a song of birthdays
Love is in the air
Greetings and good wishes
For you everywhere

025.

SING A SONG OF SISTERS

"Happy birthday, dear sister, happy birthday to you!"

This cheery tribute has accompanied the passage of another year for as long as we can remember. Where did it come from? It isn't a folk song, a nursery rhyme, or a medieval madrigal. It is simply the most popular song in the world. And it was written by a set of sisters.

Every morning, Mildred J. and Patty Smith Hill welcomed the children to their Louisville classroom with a simple four-line song. Mildred, the music teacher—a church organist, concert pianist, and an expert on Negro spirituals—had written the melody. Patty, the school's principal, had written the words. The sisters' greeting was published in *Song Stories of the Kindergarten* in 1893, and copyrighted. It was called "Good Morning to All."

From its innocent origins in kindergarten, the dear little song went on to a complicated and controversial future. It appeared in numerous songbooks under various titles with assorted verses. Somewhere along the way, the birthday lyrics were added, and the world joined the party.

In 1933, as thousands cheered, "Happy Birthday" made it to Broadway in Irving Berlin's smash musical *As Thousands Cheer*. Tsk-tsk, scolded the uncredited Hills. Enough was enough. Jessica Hill, another sister, sued for copyright infringement in August 1934 and won. The little tune was now big business.

As Thousands Cheer chucked it, but *Panama Hattie, The Male Animal*, and *The Band Wagon* picked it up. In *Happy Birthday*, Anita Loos's 1946 comedy, Helen Hayes shouted—but did not sing—it. Western Union dropped the song from its repertoire like a hot potato, and, in February 1941, instead began offering birthday telegrams crooned to the tune of "Mary Had a Little Lamb" or "Yankee Doodle," which were safely in the public domain.

As for the unsung sisters, Mildred died at the age of fifty-seven in 1916, long before her catchy little tune caught on. Patty moved to New York, became a leader in progressive education at Columbia University, and died at the age of seventy-eight in 1946.

Birthday in and birthday out, year after year after year, their melody lingers on. On stage and screen—until the copyright expires in the year 2010—singing "Happy Birthday to You" requires a royalty payment to the publisher, Summy-Burchard, every single time. When we sing it at our own party, however, it's free and clear.

Put on your party hat! Set out the cake and candles! Along with Gypsy, June, Jackie, Lee, Gloria, Thelma, Ann, Abigail, Sadie, Bessie, Jayne, Joan, Violet, Daisy, Dorothy, Lillian, Laverne, Maxene, Patty, Patience, Prudence, Yvonne, Annette, Cécile, Emilie, Marie, and all the others we've come to celebrate, we look to the Hills and sing a song of sisters!

Acknowledgments

We are deeply grateful to John H. Davis, who led us to his mother, Maude Bouvier Davis; Oscar Andrew Hammerstein, who was fruitful in the Cherry Sisters search; Vicki Gold Levi, who brought us the Hiltons from the Atlantic City Boardwalk; Howard and Ron Mandelbaum at Photofest, whose movie knowledge knows no bounds; Tom Todd, whose camera is always in focus. Also to Niki Berg, Adina Cohen, Faith Coleman, Laura Margolin Johnson, Carol Kranowitz, Judy Parker, Paula Rubenstein, Katie Stern, Barbara Strauch, Nancy Weber—and, always, the New York Society Library.

For their kind help, we thank Valerie Berney at the Public Library of Charlotte & Mecklenburg County in Charlotte, North Carolina; Ann Bowers at the Center for Archival Collections at Bowling Green State University in Bowling Green, Ohio; Jocelyn Clapp at The Bettmann Archive in New York; Evelyne Z. Daitz at The Witkin Gallery in New York; Fred Dahlinger at Circus World Museum

in Baraboo, Wisconsin; Marie-Helene Gold at the Schlesinger Library of Radcliffe College in Cambridge, Massachusetts; Paul Graves at the Holyoke Public Library in Holyoke, Massachusetts; Ryan Hayter at Hallmark Cards in Kansas City, Missouri; Shaner Magalhaes at the State Historical Society of Iowa in Iowa City, Iowa; David Ment at Teachers College Library of Columbia University in New York; Jimmy and Fay Rodolfos of the Dionne Quint Collectors in Woburn, Massachusetts; James Taylor of Atomic Books in Baltimore, Maryland, and Heather C. Wager at Orchard House in Concord, Massachusetts.

For taking such good care of our book from cover to cover, we thank our agents, Barbara Hogenson and Marcy Posner; our editor, Claire Wachtel; our designer, Leah Carlson, and the indispensable Tracy Quinn. And for taking such good care of us, we thank our husbands, Charles Hirsch and Peter Stern.

Picture Credits

UNLESS OTHERWISE NOTED HERE, ALL POSTCARDS, SHEET MUSIC, AND OTHER EPHEMERAL MATERIALS ARE FROM THE AUTHORS' COLLECTIONS.

Introduction SISTER DEAREST

Margolin sisters: Photograph by Ben Margolin
Stock sisters: Photograph by Robert E. Baker
Delany sisters: Photograph by Marianne
    Barcellona
Maude Bouvier Davis: Photograph by Niki Berg
Jacket cover from *One Special Summer* by
    Jacqueline and Lee Bouvier. Copyright ©
    1974. Used by permission of Dell Books, a
    division of Bantam Doubleday Dell
    Publishing Group, Inc.
Boyd twins: Courtesy of Jayne and Joan Boyd

One FABLED SISTERS

The Heliades (tree nymphs): Rare Books and
    Manuscript Division, The New York Public
    Library, Astor, Lenox and Tilden Foundations
Little Women (1949) poster and *Little Women* (1994)
    photograph: Photofest
My Sister Eileen: Photofest/Jagarts
Hannah and Her Sisters: Photofest
Little Women cards: Courtesy of Hallmark Cards,
    Kansas City, Mo.

Two DOUBLE TAKE

Twin nuns: Photograph by Mark Haven
Ann Landers and Abigail Van Buren:
    Corbis-Bettmann
Stowe twins: The Schlesinger Library,
    Radcliffe College
Bouvier twins with dog: Courtesy of
    Maude Bouvier Davis
Bouvier twins painting by Alfred Herter:
    Photograph by Niki Berg
Doublemint car card by Otis Shepard and
    Doublemint twins photograph: Courtesy
    of the Wm. Wrigley Jr. Company
The Young Girls of Rochefort: Photofest

Three SISTER ACT

Dolly Sisters: Apeda Studios; courtesy of The
    Witkin Gallery Inc., New York
Gumm Sisters: Photofest
Gishes and Griffith: Corbis-Bettmann
Cherry Sisters: State Historical Society of Iowa

Four MARCH OF THE SIAMESE
TWINS

Chang and Eng with wives and sons: Circus
    World Museum
Millie-Christine poster: Circus World Museum
Blazek Sisters with son (photograph): Circus
    World Museum
Gibb Sisters with dolls: Corbis-Bettmann
Hilton Sisters tooting: Circus World Museum
Hilton Sisters priming: The Vicki Gold Levi
    Collection

Five A QUINTESSENCE OF
QUINTUPLETS

Reunion: Photofest/Jagarts

Bibliography

Abbe, Kathryn McLaughlin, and Frances McLaughlin Gill. *Twins on Twins*. New York: Clarkson N. Potter, Inc., 1980.

Alcott, Louisa May. *Life, Letters, and Journals*, edited by Ednah D. Cheney. Boston: Little, Brown and Company, 1928.

Barker, Lillian. *The Dionne Legend*. Garden City, N.Y.: Doubleday and Company, Inc., 1950.

Bernard, Charles. "Circusiana." *Hobbies* magazine, July 1937.

Bernays, Edward L. *Biography of an Idea*. New York: Simon & Schuster, 1965.

Berton, Pierre. *The Dionne Years*. New York: W. W. Norton and Company Inc., 1977.

Birmingham, Stephen. *Duchess*. Boston: Little, Brown and Company, 1981.

Blatz, William. *The Five Sisters*. New York: William Morrow and Company, 1938.

Blatz, William, et al. *Collected Studies on the Dionne Quintuplets*. St. George's School for Child Study at the University of Toronto. Toronto: The University of Toronto Press, 1937.

Bogdan, Robert. *Freak Show*. Chicago: The University of Chicago Press, 1988.

Bouvier, Jacqueline and Lee. *One Special Summer*. New York: Delacorte Press, 1974.

Brough, James with Annette, Cécile, Marie, and Yvonne Dionne. *We Were Five*. New York: Simon & Schuster, 1965.

Brown, Eve. *Champagne Cholly*. New York: E. P. Dutton and Company, Inc., 1947.

Buckley, Christopher. "You Got a Problem?" *The New Yorker*, December 4, 1995.

Bryan, J., III, and Charles J. V. Murphy. *The Windsor Story*. New York: William Morrow and Company, Inc., 1979.

Churchill, Allen. *The Upper Crust*. Englewood Cliffs, N.J.: Prentice-Hall, Inc., 1970.

Chusid, Irwin. "Cherry Bomb." *New York Press*, November 13–19, 1996.

Cone, Fairfax M. *With All Its Faults*. Boston: Little, Brown and Company, 1969.

Davis, John H. *The Bouviers: From Waterloo to the Kennedys and Beyond*. Washington, D.C.: National Press Books, 1993.

———. *The Bouviers: Portrait of an American Family*. New York: Farrar, Straus & Giroux, 1969.

Delany, Sarah L., with Amy Hill Hearth. *On My Own at 107*. San Francisco: HarperSanFrancisco, 1997.

Delany, Sarah and A. Elizabeth, with Amy Hill Hearth. *Having Our Say: The Delany Sisters' First 100 Years*. New York: Kodansha International, 1993.

———. *The Delany Sisters' Book of Everyday Wisdom*. New York: Kodansha International, 1994.

Drimmer, Frederick. *Very Special People*. New York: Amjon Publishers, Inc., 1973.

Dunne, Dominick. "Gloria's Euphoria." *Fatal Charms*. New York: Crown Publishers, Inc., 1987.

Edwards, Anne. *Judy Garland*. New York: Simon & Schuster, 1974.

Ellis, Edward S., M.A. *1000 Mythological Characters Briefly Described*. New York: Hinds & Noble, 1895.

Ewen, David. *All the Years of American Popular Music*. Englewood Cliffs, N.J.: Prentice-Hall, Inc., 1977.

Farnsworth, Marjorie. *The Ziegfeld Follies*. London: Peter Davies, 1956.

Fiedler, Leslie. *Freaks*. New York: Simon & Schuster, 1978.

Fishel, Elizabeth. *Sisters*. New York: William Morrow and Company, Inc., 1979.

Fontaine, Joan. *No Bed of Roses*. New York: William Morrow and Company, Inc., 1978.

Gardiner, Juliet. *The Brontës at Haworth*. Great Britain: Collins and Brown Limited, 1992, New York: Clarkson N. Potter, Inc., 1992.

Gayley, Charles Mills, Litt.D., LL.D. *The Classic Myths in English Literature and in Art*. Boston: Ginn and Company, 1939.

Gilbert, Douglas. *American Vaudeville*. New York: Whittlesey House, 1940.

Ginzberg, Henry. *Legends of the Bible*. New York: Simon & Schuster, 1956.

Gish, Lillian. *Dorothy and Lillian Gish*. New York: Charles Scribner's Sons, 1973.

———. *The Movies, Mr. Griffith and Me*. Englewood Cliffs, N.J.: Prentice-Hall, Inc., 1969.

Goodrum, Charles, and Helen Dalrymple. *Advertising in America: The First 200 Years*. New York: Harry N. Abrams, Inc., 1990.

Grimal, Pierre. *The Dictionary of Classical Mythology*, translated by A. R. Maxwell-Hyslop. Oxford: Basil Blackwell Publisher, 1986.

Guerber, H. A. *The Myths of Greece and Rome*. London: George G. Harrap and Co. Ltd., 1907.

Halliwell, Leslie. *Halliwell's Film Guide*. 3d Edition. New York: Charles Scribner's Sons, 1981.

Havoc, June. *Early Havoc*. New York: Dell, 1959.

Hedrick, Joan D. *Harriet Beecher Stowe*. New York: Oxford University Press, 1994.

Higham, Charles. *Bette: The Life of Bette Davis*. New York: Macmillan, 1981.

———. *The Duchess of Windsor*. New York: McGraw-Hill Book Company, 1988.

———. *Sisters*. New York: Coward-McCann, Inc., 1984.

Hilton, Daisy and Violet. *Intimate Lives and Loves of the Hilton Sisters*, excerpted in James Taylor's *Shocked and Amazed! On and Off the Midway*. Baltimore: Atomic Books, 1996.

Howells, Mildred, ed. *Life in Letters of William Dean Howells*, vol. II. Garden City, N.J.: Doubleday, Doran and Company, Inc., 1928.

Lash, John. *Twins and the Double*. London: Thames and Hudson Ltd., 1993.

Laurie, Joe, Jr. *Vaudeville: From the Honky-Tonks to the Palace*. New York: Henry Holt and Company, 1953.

Leaming, Barbara. *Bette Davis*. New York: Simon & Schuster, 1992.

Lee, Gypsy Rose. *Gypsy*. New York: Harper & Brothers, Publishers, 1957.

Malden, Mrs. Charles. *Jane Austen*. Boston: Roberts Brothers, 1889.

Menninger, William C., M.D., et al. *How to Help Your Children: The Parents' Handbook*. New York: Sterling Publishing Co., Inc., 1959.

Murray, Alexander S. *Manual of Mythology*. New York: Scribner, Welford, and Armstrong, 1874.

Myerson, Joel, and Daniel Shealy, eds.; Madeleine B. Stern, associate ed. *The Selected Letters of Louisa May Alcott*. Boston: Little, Brown and Company, 1987.

Pilat, Olivier, and Jo Ranson. *Sodom by the Sea*. Garden City, N.Y.: Garden City Publishing Co., Inc., 1941.

Quirk, Lawrence J. *Fasten Your Seat Belts*. New York: William Morrow and Company, Inc., 1990.

Ross, Irwin. *The Image Merchants*. Garden City, N.Y.: Doubleday and Co., Inc., 1959.

Ross, Ishbel. *Charmers and Cranks*. New York: Harper & Row, 1965.

Roth, Lillian. *I'll Cry Tomorrow*. New York: Frederick Fell, Inc., 1954.

St. John, Adela Rogers. *The Honeycomb*. Garden City, N.Y.: Doubleday and Company, Inc., 1969.

Sampson, Henry T. *Blacks in Blackface*. Metuchen, N.J.: Scarecrow Press, Inc., 1980.

Samuels, Charles and Louise. *Once upon a Stage*. New York: Dodd, Mead and Company, 1974.

Schessler, Ken. *This Is Hollywood*. Los Angeles: Universal Books, 1978.

Sherwood, Robert Edmund. *Hold Yer Hosses!* New York: Macmillan, 1932.

Shipman, David. *The Great Movie Stars: The Golden Years*. New York: Bonanza Books, 1970.

———. *Judy Garland: The Secret Life of an American Legend*. New York: Hyperion, 1992.

Slide, Anthony. *Selected Vaudeville Criticism*. Metuchen, N.J.: Scarecrow Press, Inc., 1988.

———. *The Vaudevillians*. New York: Arlington House, Crown 1981.

Soucy, Jean-Yves, with Annette, Cécile, and Yvonne Dionne. *Family Secrets*. New York: Berkley Books, 1997.

Spada, James. *More Than a Woman: An Intimate Biography of Bette Davis*. New York: Bantam, 1993.

Spaeth, Sigmund. *A History of Popular Music in America*. New York: Random House, 1948.

Stine, Whitney. *Mother Goddam*. New York: Hawthorn Books, Inc., 1974.

Twain, Mark. "Personal Habits of the Siamese Twins." *Mark Twain's Sketches, New and Old*. American Publishing Company, 1875.

Van Buren, Abigail. *The Best of Dear Abby*. New York: Pocket Books, 1981.

Vanderbilt, Gloria, and Lady Thelma Furness. *Double Exposure*. New York: David McKay Company, Inc., 1958.

Walker, Barbara G. *The Woman's Dictionary of Symbols and Sacred Objects*. San Francisco: Harper & Row, 1988.

Wallace, Irving, and Amy Wallace. *The Two*. New York: Simon & Schuster, 1978.

Wright, Lawrence. "Double Mystery." *The New Yorker*, August 7, 1995.

Index

NUMBERS IN ITALICS REFER TO PHOTOGRAPHS